# Bennett Cerf's Houseful of Laughter

# Bennett Cerf's
# Houseful

Random House New York

# of Laughter

*Illustrated by Arnold Roth , Walt Kelly, and Roger Price*

**The editor thanks the following for permission to reprint copyrighted material:** McGraw-Hill Book Co., Inc., for an excerpt from *It All Started With Columbus*, revised edition, by Richard Armour, copyright, 1953 © 1961, by Richard Armour; Heywood Hale Broun and Constance Broun for "The Fifty-First Dragon," copyright, 1921, 1941, by Heywood Hale Broun; Simon and Schuster, Inc., for "The Story of Chicken Little," copyright, 1953, by Walt Kelly; Helen Thurber for "The Little Girl and the Wolf" by James Thurber, copyright, 1939, by The New Yorker Magazine, Inc.; Doubleday & Company, Inc., for "The Ransom of Red Chief" from *Whirligigs* by O. Henry, copyright, 1907, by Doubleday & Company, Inc.; Random House, Inc., for "How Beautiful With Mud" from *We Shook the Family Tree* by Hildegarde Dolson, copyright, 1941, 1942, 1946, by Hildegarde Dolson; McIntosh and Otis, Inc., for "The Affair at 7, Rue de M—," copyright © 1955, by John Steinbeck; Alfred A. Knopf, Inc., for "Father Opens My Mail" from *Life With Father*, copyright, 1934, by Clarence Day; Dodd, Mead & Company for "How We Kept Mother's Day" from *Laugh With Leacock* by Stephen Leacock, copyright, 1930, by Dodd, Mead & Company; Harper & Row, Publishers, Incorporated, for "Your Boy and His Dog" from *Chips Off the Old Benchley* by Robert Benchley, copyright, 1932, by The Hearst Corporation, New York Mirror Division; Simon and Schuster, Inc., for droodles from *The Rich Sardine*, copyright, 1954, by Roger Price; World Publishing Company for "Pay the Two Francs," copyright ©1960, by Art Buchwald, from *Don't Forget to Write;* Billy Rose for "Learning to Drive" from *Wine, Women, and Words*, copyright, 1946, 1947, 1948, by Glenmore Productions, Inc.; Hughes Mearns for "The Little Man Who Wasn't There"; John Schaffner Literary Agent for "Miniature" from *For Partly Proud Parents* (Harper & Brothers), copyright, 1950, by Richard Armour; Simon and Schuster, Inc., for "Infant Prodigy" from *Look Who's a Mother*, copyright, 1945, by Margaret Fishback; E. P. Dutton & Co., Inc., for "Habits of the Hippopotamus" from *Gaily the Troubadour* by Arthur Guiterman, copyright, 1936, by E. P. Dutton & Co., Inc.; Little, Brown and Co. for "Eletelephony" from *Tirra Lirra* by Laura E. Richards; Liveright, Publishers, New York, for three poems from *Poems in Praise of Practically Nothing* by Samuel Hoffenstein, copyright © R-1956, by David Hoffenstein; The Dial Press, Inc., for "Song of the Pop-Bottlers" from *A Bowl of Bishop* by Morris Bishop, copyright, 1954, by Morris Bishop; Little, Brown and Co. for "The Lama," copyright, 1931, by Ogden Nash (originally published in *The New Yorker*), "Song of the Open Road," copyright, 1932, by Ogden Nash (originally published in *The New Yorker*), "Reflections on Babies," copyright, 1940, by Ogden Nash, and "The Termite," "The Fly," and "The Eel," copyright, 1942, by Ogden Nash; Harper & Row, Publishers, Incorporated, for limericks from *Out on a Limerick*, copyright © 1960, by Bennett Cerf; Epstein and Carroll, Associates, for "The Word Market" from *The Phantom Tollbooth* by Norton Juster, copyright © 1961, by Norton Juster; Helen Thurber for "The Night the Bed Fell" by James Thurber, copyright, 1933, © 1961, by The New Yorker Magazine, Inc.; Doubleday & Company, Inc., for "The Face Is Familiar But—" copyright, 1945, by Max Shulman, from *The Many Loves of Dobie Gillis* by Max Shulman; Random House, Inc., for "Practice Mission" from *No Time for Sergeants* by Mac Hyman, copyright, 1954, by Mac Hyman.

The riddles in "Riddle-de-Dee" are reprinted from *Riddle-de-Dee* by Bennett Cerf (Random House), copyright © 1962, by Bennett Cerf.

 Published in New York by Random House, Inc., and simultaneously in Toronto, Canada, by Random House of Canada, Limited. Manufactured in the United States of America.

Library of Congress catalog card number: 63-14748

# Contents

# Foreword

HOUSEFUL OF LAUGHTER is one anthology that changed stories in midstream—and is, I promise you, very much the better for it. Originally, it consisted of material *I* believed would tickle the fancies of boys and girls in their early teens. Several mothers and fathers approved my selections. "Off to the printers with the script!" I cried happily.

Then, at the last moment, I had a revolutionary idea. Why not, I suggested at an editorial meeting, astonishing associates with my ingenuity, test our material on the boys and girls *themselves*—to find out if they still respond to stories that once convulsed their tottering old parents?

Testers proved easy to come by. Anthologists and critics evidently mature early in life—with opinions that are frighteningly definite. Nary a 12-to-15-year-old did we encounter who didn't know *exactly* what should be included in HOUSEFUL OF LAUGHTER—and, equally important, what should be left out. Kitty Hart's lovely daughter, Cathy, and precocious and persuasive Tommy and Peter Bernstein were particularly helpful. My own two boys remembered stories they had loved when they were younger. Everybody got into the act. *And did we listen?*

As the book changed form, I grew so enthusiastic about the help of my young collaborators that my wife predicted I'd wind up in schoolyards hissing at teenagers, "Psst! Want to help edit an anthology of humor?"

The fact is that everybody *wants* to laugh more in this world today—and everybody *needs* to if he is to preserve his sanity. HOUSEFUL OF LAUGHTER in its final form, will, I hope, at least point some thousands of young readers in the right direction.

BENNETT CERF

# Bennett Cerf's Houseful of Laughter

# It All Started With Columbus

*by Richard Armour*

## The Discovery of America

America was founded by Columbus in 1492. This is an easy date to remember because it rhymes with "ocean blue," which was the color of the Atlantic in those days. If he had sailed a year later the date would still be easy to remember because it would rhyme with "boundless sea."

Columbus fled to this country because of persecution by Ferdinand and Isabella, who refused to believe the world was round, even when Columbus showed them an egg. Ferdinand later became famous because he objected to bullfights and said he preferred to smell flowers if he had to smell anything. He was stung in the end by a bee.

Before Columbus reached America, which he named after a man called American Vesuvius, he cried "Ceylon! Ceylon!" because he wanted to see India, which was engraved on his heart, before he died. When he arrived, he cried again. This time he cried "Excelsior!" meaning "I have founded it." Excelsior has been widely used ever since by persons returning with chinaware from China, with indiaware from India, and with underware from Down Under.

Columbus was mistaken in thinking he had reached India when actually he had not got even as far as Indiana. There is still a great

---

From the book *It All Started With Columbus*.

deal of confusion about the East and the West. As Columbus discovered, if you go west long enough you find yourself in the east, and vice versa. The East and the West are kept apart by the Date Line, just as the North and South are kept apart by the Masons' Dixon Line. In the New World most of the eastern half of the country is called the Middle West, although it is known as the East by those who live in the Far West.

Columbus, who was as confused as anybody who has been at sea for a long time, called the first people he saw "Indians." It is not known what they called Columbus. His unfortunate error has been perpetuated through the centuries. The original Americans are still known as "Indians," while all manner of immigrants from England, Ireland, Angora, and Lichtenstein are referred to as "Americans."[1]

Accompanied by his devoted followers, the Knights of Columbus, Columbus made several other voyages in search of India. Try as he might, however, he kept discovering America, and finally returned to Spain to die. He lived for a time in Madrid, but spent his last days in Disgrace.

---

[1] Or, by their mathematically inclined friends, "100 percent Americans."

## A MINORITY OPINION

Some say it was not Columbus who discovered America but a man named Leaf Ericson. Leaf came from one of the Scandinavian countries with a shipload of people, all of whom were called Yon Yonson or Ole Olson or Big Swede, and went straight to Wisconsin, where he unloaded his passengers and went back for more.

On his next trip he went to Minnesota.

We know all this from some undecipherable remarks he made on a piece of stone. This stone has since become an utter rune.

## FURTHER EXPLORATIONS

After Columbus proved the world was round, a great many people went around it. Marco Polo, who was one of the earlier explorers, had the misfortune to live several centuries before Columbus. Therefore, although he got around a good deal, he did not get completely around. He went far to the north, however, and is remembered for his discovery of the Polo regions.

The chief rivals in exploration were England and Spain. England had men like Cabot, who spoke only to a man named Lowell, and Sir Francis Drake, who had a singed beard and a ship called the *Golden Behind.*

Nor should we forget Sir Martin Fourflusher.[1]

The struggle between England and Spain came to a climax in an epic sea battle off the Azores known as the Last Fight of the Revenge. In this decisive conflict, Sir Richard Grenville and Alfred Lord Tennyson proved conclusively that the lighter English warships could get more miles to the galleon.

England has ruled the waves ever since and has kept the sun from

---

[1] A direct descendant of the early Saxons, who knew all the Angles.

setting anywhere on her empire, thus providing a longer working day than in other countries.

### STILL FURTHER EXPLORATIONS

Other explorers included Bilbo, Cabbage de Vaca, Cortez (known as The Stout, who traveled much in realms looking for gold), and Pantsy de Lion, a thirsty old man who was looking for a drinking fountain.[1] He never found it, but he founded Florida, to which a great many thirsty old men have gone ever since.

## The Virginia Colony

All this time there was not much happening in the New World, except that it was steadily growing older.

This period, known as the Doldrums, came to an end in fifteen-something-or-other when Sir Walter Raleigh, a man with a pointed beard and a pointless way of muddying his cloak, established a colony in America in the hope of pleasing the Queen, whose favor he had been in but was temporarily out of.

Although he claimed the new land in the name of Elizabeth, he called it Virginia, which aroused suspicions in Elizabeth's mind and caused her to confine Sir Walter in a tower. While imprisoned, Sir Walter made good use of his time by writing a history of the world on such scraps of paper as he could find, and filling other scraps of paper with a weed brought back from Virginia.

He had barely completed his history when he lost his head. Had he been permitted to keep it a few years longer he might have become the first man to roll a cigarette with one hand.

The Virginia Colony was lost for a time, and its name was

---

[1] Some historians say that in his wanderings through the South he invented the Dixie cup, just in case.

changed to The Lost Colony, but it was subsequently found at about the place where it was last seen. Its original name of Virginia was restored because Elizabeth no longer cared, being dead.[1]

## THE INDIANS

The people who were already in the New World when the white men arrived were the first Americans, or America Firsters. They were also referred to as the First Families of Virginia.

The early colonists found the Indians living in toupees, or wigwams, and sending up smoke signals, or wigwags, with piece pipes. Apparently because of a shortage of pipes, they sat in a circle and passed one pipe around, each biting off a piece as it passed. The chief Indian was named Hiawatha, and his squaw, whose name was Evangeline, did all the work. This was later to become an Old American Custom.

The Chiefs, it must be said in all fairness, were too busy to work. They were engaged in making wampum, or whoopee, when they were not mixing war paint or scattering arrowheads about, to be found centuries later.

In order to have their hands free to work, the squaws carried their babies, or cabooses, on their back, very much as kangaroos carry their babies on their front, only different.

The Indians were stern, silent people who never showed their feelings, even while being scalped. They crept up on their enemies without breaking a twig and were familiar with all the warpaths. Despite their savage ways, they sincerely loved peace, and were called Nobel Savages.

Their favorite word was "How," which the colonists soon learned was not a question.

The whites feared the redskins and considered them the forest's

---

[1] The end of Elizabeth is known as the Elizabethan Period.

prime evil. Some went so far as to say that "The only good Indian is a wooden Indian." The redskins resented the whiteskins because they thought they had come to take their lands away from them, and their fears were well grounded.

Captain John Smith was the first of a long line of Smiths who came to this country to keep up with the Joneses.

He was captured by the great Indian Chief, Powhatan, and was about to be killed when Popocatepetl, the fiery young daughter of the Chief, stepped in. We are not told what she stepped in, but she saved Captain John Smith's life, for which he thanked her. Later she married an Englishman, which improved relations.

## The Pilgrims

The Pilgrims were a branch of the Puritans, and were proud of their family tree. They wore tall hats, which they had to take off when they went inside because they attended a low church. This displeased King James, who raised the roof. He demanded that they attend the same church as he did. At least this is his side of the story, which became known as the King James Version.

Although the King insisted, the Puritans, who were very stiff-necked from years of wearing truffles on their collars, stubbornly declined. They would probably still be declining if they had not left England and gone to Leyden, a city in Holland noted for the discovery of electricity in a jar. (Electricity was subsequently lost for a while, but was rediscovered, by accident, when Benjamin Franklin was told to go fly a kite, and did.)

While in Holland, the Pilgrims suffered from pangs of sin, and sent their children to Dutch Reform Schools when they misbehaved. These children, naturally enough, became Protestants, but their protests were ignored.

## THE PLYMOUTH COLONY

After several years in Holland, the Pilgrims decided to set out for the New World. This decision to move is known as Pilgrims' Progress.

The ship on which they sailed was the *Mayflower*. In stormy weather the women and children descended below the heaving decks, thus becoming the *Mayflower* descendants. There they huddled with the Colonial Dames and other early settlers and passed the weary hours comparing genealogies.

It was a long and perilous voyage across the Atlantic. Several times they were blown off their course. But finally, in 1620, which was a doubly Memorable Year because it was also the year in which they set sail, they sighted the rocky coast. The rock on which they landed they called Plymouth Rock because it reminded them of another rock of the same name in England. They built a small picket fence around it and made it a national shrine.

The first four men ashore became our fourfathers.

## THE FIRST WINTER

After a short stay on Plymouth Rock, which was windy and damp, the Pilgrims sought a more sheltered place to build a town. One party went in one direction and one went in another. This was the beginning of the two-party system. When the two parties met, they held the first town meeting.

The first winter was cold, which was a distinct surprise to the Pilgrims. Indeed, they might not have survived but for the corn that was given them by friendly Indians. By a curious quirk of history, it has since become illegal for white men to give Indians either corn or rye.

The next spring the crops were good, and in the fall the Pilgrims celebrated their first Thanksgiving, which fell, that fall, on a Thursday. The friendly Indians were invited, and the unfriendly Indians stayed in the background, muttering.

One of the leaders of the little band[1] at Plymouth was Captain Miles Standish. He was known throughout the township for his courtship.

He was an exceptional man. Except for him, almost all the Pilgrims were named William or John. One of the latter was Miles Standish's friend, quiet John Alden, a man who did not speak for himself until spoken to. He was spoken to, and sharply, by the fair Priscilla, whom he married, much to the annoyance of Miles Standish, who thought he was stood up by his stand-in.

## The Colonies Grow

Let us leave the Pilgrims in Plymouth and see what was happening elsewhere in New England.

Education took a forward step with the founding of Harvard in a yard near the Charles River. Among the early benefactors of Harvard was a plantation owner from the South known as "Cotton" Mather. The first library was only a five-foot shelf, given to the college by T. S. Eliot, a graduate who no longer had need of it. The books on this shelf are known as the Great Books and have grown to one hundred.

With the founding of two other old colleges, Old Eli and Old

---

[1] A precursor of such bandleaders as Paul Whiteman and Benny Goodman.

Nassau, the educational system was complete. Because of the ivory towers which were a distinctive feature of many of the early buildings, the three colleges became known as the Ivory League.

To provide recreational facilities for students at Harvard, the city of Boston was established. Boston became famous for its two famous hills, Beacon and Bunker, its two famous churches, North and South, and its two famous bays, Back and Front.

The people of Boston became wealthy by exporting baked beans and codfish, which they were smart enough not to eat themselves. Many, who were pillars of the churches and pillars of society, came to be known as Propper Bostonians.

## WILLIAMS AND PENN

One who was unhappy with life in Plymouth was Roger Williams, who thought the Pilgrims were intolerable. The Pilgrims, in turn, thought Williams was impossible. He proposed that they pay the Indians for their land instead of simply taking it from them. This utopian suggestion was dismissed by the Pilgrims as economically unsound.

Because of his unorthodox views, the Pilgrims branded him. They branded him a heretic, and drove him from town to town, although he preferred to walk. This was why Roger Williams reluctantly left Plymouth and founded Rhode Island, which is really not an island and is so small that it is usually indicated on maps by the letters "R.I." out in the Atlantic Ocean. It was once densely wooded. It is now densely populated.

William Penn, on the other hand, came to America to collect some land the King owed his father. He belonged to a frightened religious sect known as the Quakers. So that he would not be forgotten, he gave his name to the Pennsylvania Railroad, the Pennsylvania Station, and the state prison, which is known as the Penn.

## MASSACHUSETTS BAY

The English had always been a seafaring race, ever since they were Danes. Therefore one of their first acts in the New World was to make Massachusetts Bay a colony. From Massachusetts Bay and the nearby bayous they went out in their high-masted vessels looking for whale oil, which they found mostly in whales. The men who went away on voyages to capture whales were called whalers. So, by coincidence, were their sturdy ships. This is more confusing to us now than it was then.

The most famous whale, in those days, was an ill-tempered, unpredictable old whale called Moody Dick. Everyone was on the lookout for him, especially whalers whose legs he had bitten off in one of his nastier moods. The one-legged whaler who was most resentful was Captain A. Hab, who persisted until he finally managed to harpoon Moody Dick where it hurt the most. The whale had the last word, however, for he overturned Captain A. Hab's ship, the *Peapod*, which went down with all hands, including both of Captain A. Hab's.

## CONNECTICUT

Fortunately for those who liked to visit New York but preferred not to live there, Connecticut was founded within commuting distance.

It was founded by Thomas Hooker, a clergyman who, in a dim church, interpreted the Gospel according to his own lights. He would also accept no money for his preaching, which set a low wage standard for others; he was therefore scorned as a free thinker. So he left under a cloud. Many of his parishioners believed his stern words about hell and followed him to Hartford, where he guaranteed them protection in the hereafter and sold them the first fire-insurance policies.

Connecticut is usually spelled Conn, which is easier.

## Life in Old New England

Most of the Puritans were ministers. Each week they could hardly wait until Sunday, when they preached for several hours on such subjects as "Hellfire" and "Damnation." In those days, church attendance was as good every Sunday as it is today on Easter.

The homes of the Puritans were simple and austere, but their furniture was antique and therefore frightfully expensive. The chairs were as straight and stiff as the Puritans themselves, and had hard bottoms. They became known as period pieces because they went to pieces after a short period of sitting on them.

Stores were known as Shoppes, or Ye Olde Shoppes. Prices were somewhat higher at the latter.

The Puritans believed in justice. A woman who was a witch, or a man who was a son of a witch, was punished by being stuck in the stocks. These were wooden devices that had holes to put the arms and legs through, and were considered disgraceful. They were also considered uncomfortable.

Every day the men went out into the fields in their blunderbusses and sowed corn. The women, meanwhile, were busy at home embroidering the alphabet and the date on a piece of cloth.

Other amusements were pillories, whipping posts, and Indian massacres.

### THE LAND

The land was stony and hilly, except in places where it was hilly and stony. The stones were useful for making millstones and milestones. The Indians sharpened them and used them for scalping and other social purposes.

The hills were useful to watch for Indians from, unless the Indians were already on them. They were hard to plow up, but they were relatively easy to plow down.

THE CLIMATE

The winters in New England were long. Largely for this reason, the summers were short. In keeping with the seasons, long underwear was worn in the winter and short underwear in the summer.

## The Dutch and the French Come to America

Many believed there was a shorter way to get to Asia than around America. Not yet having discovered the Panama Canal, they were looking for the next best thing, which was the Northwest Passage. Since it did not exist, it was, of course, hard to find. Nevertheless many Intrepid Explorers made their reputation hunting for it.

One of those who sought the Northwest Passage was Henry Hudson. In a ship of which he was part owner, called the *Half Mine,* he led a crew of Dutchmen to the mouth of the Hudson River, which he was pleased to find named after himself.

Stopping only to make friends with the Indians and to buy the island of Manhattan from an Indian named Minnehaha (or "Laughing Minnie") for a handful of beads,[1] he pushed on up the river. When he stopped pushing he was in Albany, and he was disappointed. The water was getting shallower and shallower and it was clear. It was clear that this was not the Northwest Passage, and that instead of founding an important route to the Orient, he was about to founder at the state capital. The choice was also clear. He must remain in Albany or make the hard and perilous voyage back across the Atlantic. Without hesitation he chose the latter.

On a second trip to the New World in search of the elusive Passage, Henry Hudson sailed into Hudson Bay. This, again, was not the Northwest Passage, but its name had a familiar ring.

It is not known what became of this Able Navigator who had not been able to find what he was looking for. One theory is that Hudson met Cadillac and De Soto, and that together they discovered Detroit.

## NEW AMSTERDAM

Because of Henry Hudson's explorations, the Dutch laid claim to the mouth of the Hudson River, which in their systematic way they divided into the North River and the East River. A stubborn race, they named Manhattan New Amsterdam, although it was obviously New York.

New Amsterdam was soon swarming with wealthy Dutch traitors known as poltroons. These were bluff, hearty men who smoked long pipes and loved to eat burghers. They frequently had their pictures painted, and one of the most picturesque was their Governor, Rip Van Winkle, a one-legged gentleman who fell into a deep sleep while watching a bowling game.

The English also claimed Manhattan, in view of the fact the beads with which it was purchased were plainly stamped "Made in

---

[1] Beads were then selling at $24 a handful.

England." The Dutch could not see the merits of their claim, but they could see that the English had more guns on their warships, so they left.

This was a turning point.

The clever English changed the name Amsterdam to York, but they retained the New.[1]

## LA SALLE

The French, although exhausted by the Hundred Years' War, were not too tired to try to establish themselves in the New World. There were still mountains which had not been planted with flags, and there were still rivers that had not been sailed up. So they sailed up them. Many of these still rivers ran deep and led into fastnesses where no white man had ever trod and very few had walked.

At last the only river remaining to be sailed up was the Mississippi. In this instance the French explorer La Salle defied convention. A headstrong young man, he began at the headwaters of the mighty river and sailed down it. He thus not only opened up a vast new territory but discovered an easier means of navigating the rivers of America. La Salle's interesting account of his trip down the river, called *Life on the Mississippi,* is available in an English translation by Mark Twain.

Thanks to La Salle, the Mississippi basin remained in French hands until they grew tired of holding it and sold it for $15,000,000, which many thought was a high price for a second-hand basin.

It is to the French also that we owe the establishment of the beautiful city of Quebec, which was named, according to custom, after the King of France, whose name, according to custom, was Louis (pronounced kwē̇-bĕk′). The English later seized Quebec and

---

[1] The city was later called New York, New York, for the sake of those who did not catch it the first time.

its outskirts, called Canada, from the French, but not without a struggle.

Henceforth the French were dominated by the English, who became our Good Neighbors to the north. We have had amicable relations ever since by agreeing that there are two sides to everything, for example Niagara Falls, which has an American side and a Canadian side.

## Test

1. Why do you think Columbus was so interested in traveling to distant places? What else do you know about his home life?
2. Are you really convinced that the world is round? Do you worry much about it?
3. To what extent would the course of American history have been altered if America had never been discovered?
4. What would you say about the Puritans? Would you say the same if they were listening?
5. Can the passengers on the *Mayflower* be considered immigrants? With their strong sense of duty, do you suppose they tried to conceal anything from the customs officials?
6. Have you ever thought how much of a Pilgrim was wasted when an Indian kept only his scalp?
7. Trace on a map the voyages of Henry Hudson. Use a solid line to show where he went and a dotted line to show where he thought he was going. Sign on the dotted line.
8. What would you have done if you had been in La Salle's shoes? How do you know he wore any?

# The Fifty-First Dragon

*by Heywood Broun*

Of all the pupils at the knight school Gawaine Le Coeur-Hardy was among the least promising. He was tall and sturdy, but his instructors soon discovered that he lacked spirit. He would hide in the woods when the jousting class was called, although his companions and members of the faculty sought to appeal to his better nature by shouting to him to come out and break his neck like a man. Even when they told him that the lances were padded, the horses no more than ponies and the field unusually soft for late autumn, Gawaine refused to grow enthusiastic. The Headmaster and the Assistant Professor of Pleasaunce were discussing the case one spring afternoon and the Assistant Professor could see no remedy but expulsion.

"No," said the Headmaster, as he looked out at the purple hills which ringed the school, "I think I'll train him to slay dragons."

"He might be killed," objected the Assistant Professor.

"So he might," replied the Headmaster brightly. But he added, more soberly, "We must consider the greater good. We are responsible for the formation of this lad's character."

"Are the dragons particularly bad this year?" interrupted the Assistant Professor. This was characteristic. He always seemed restive when the head of the school began to talk ethics and the ideals of the institution.

"I've never known them worse," replied the headmaster. "Up in the hills to the south last week they killed a number of peasants, two cows and a prize pig. And if this dry spell holds there's no telling

---

From *Seeing Things at Night.*

when they may start a forest fire simply by breathing around indiscriminately."

"Would any refund on the tuition fee be necessary in case of an accident to young Coeur-Hardy?"

"No," the principal answered, judicially, "that's all covered in the contract. But as a matter of fact he wouldn't be killed. Before I send him up in the hills I'm going to give him a magic word."

"That's a good idea," said the Professor. "Sometimes they work wonders."

From that day on Gawaine specialized in dragons. His course included both theory and practice. In the morning there were long lectures on the history, anatomy, manners and customs of dragons. Gawaine did not distinguish himself in these studies. He had a marvelously versatile gift for forgetting things. In the afternoon he showed to better advantage, for then he would go down to the South Meadow and practice with a battle-ax. In this exercise he was truly impressive, for he had enormous strength as well as speed and grace. He even developed a deceptive display of ferocity. Old alumni say that it was a thrilling sight to see Gawaine charging across the field toward the dummy paper dragon which had been set up for his practice. As he ran he would brandish his ax and shout "A murrain on thee!" or some other vivid bit of campus slang. It never took him more than one stroke to behead the dummy dragon.

Gradually his task was made more difficult. Paper gave way to papier-mâché and finally to wood, but even the toughest of these dummy dragons had no terrors for Gawaine. One sweep of the ax always did the business. There were those who said that when the practice was protracted until dusk and the dragons threw long, fantastic shadows across the meadow Gawaine did not charge so impetuously nor shout so loudly. It is possible there was malice in this charge. At any rate, the Headmaster decided by the end of June that it was time for the test. Only the night before a dragon had come close to the school grounds and had eaten some of the lettuce from the garden. The faculty decided that Gawaine was ready. They gave him a diploma and a new battle-ax and the Headmaster summoned him to a private conference.

"Sit down," said the Headmaster. "Have a cigarette."

Gawaine hesitated.

"Oh, I know it's against the rules," said the Headmaster. "But after all, you have received your preliminary degree. You are no longer a boy. You are a man. Tomorrow you will go out into the world, the great world of achievement."

Gawaine took a cigarette. The Headmaster offered him a match but he produced one of his own and began to puff away with a dexterity which quite amazed the principal.

"Here you have learned the theories of life," continued the Headmaster, resuming the thread of his discourse, "but after all, life is not a matter of theories. Life is a matter of facts. It calls on the young and the old alike to face these facts, even though they are hard and sometimes unpleasant. Your problem, for example, is to slay dragons."

"They say that those dragons down in the south wood are five hundred feet long," ventured Gawaine, timorously.

"Stuff and nonsense!" said the Headmaster. "The curate saw one last week from the top of Arthur's Hill. The dragon was sunning himself down in the valley. The curate didn't have an opportunity to look at him very long because he felt it was his duty to hurry back to make a report to me. He said the monster—or shall I say, the big lizard?—wasn't an inch over two hundred feet. But the size has nothing at all to do with it. You'll find the big ones even easier than the little ones. They're far slower on their feet and less aggressive, I'm told. Besides, before you go I'm going to equip you in such fashion that you need have no fear of all the dragons in the world."

"I'd like an enchanted cap," said Gawaine.

"What's that?" answered the Headmaster, testily.

"A cap to make me disappear," explained Gawaine.

The Headmaster laughed indulgently. "You mustn't believe all those old wives' stories," he said. "There isn't any such thing. A cap to make you disappear, indeed! What would you do with it? You haven't even appeared yet. Why, my boy, you could walk from here to London, and nobody would so much as look at you. You're nobody. You couldn't be more invisible than that."

Gawaine seemed dangerously close to a relapse into his old habit of whimpering. The Headmaster reassured him: "Don't worry; I'll give you something much better than an enchanted cap. I'm going to give you a magic word. All you have to do is to repeat the magic charm once and no dragon can possibly harm a hair of your head. You can cut off his head at your leisure."

He took a heavy book from the shelf behind his desk and began to run through it. "Sometimes," he said, "the charm is a whole phrase or even a sentence. I might, for instance, give you 'To make the'—no, that might not do. I think a single word would be best for dragons."

"A short word," suggested Gawaine.

"It can't be too short or it wouldn't be potent. There isn't so much hurry as all that. Here's a splendid magic word: 'Rumplesnitz.' Do you think you can learn that?"

Gawaine tried and in an hour or so he seemed to have the word well in hand. Again and again he interrupted the lesson to inquire, "And if I say 'Rumplesnitz,' the dragon can't possibly hurt me?" And always the Headmaster replied, "If you only say 'Rumplesnitz,' you are perfectly safe."

Toward morning Gawaine seemed resigned to his career. At daybreak the Headmaster saw him to the edge of the forest and pointed him to the direction on which he should proceed. About a mile away to the southwest a cloud of steam hovered over an open meadow in the woods and the Headmaster assured Gawaine that under the steam he would find whether it would be best to approach the dragon on the run as he did in his practice in the South Meadow or to walk slowly toward him, shouting "Rumplesnitz" all the way.

The problem was decided for him. No sooner had he come to the fringe of the meadow than the dragon spied him and began to charge. It was a large dragon and yet it seemed decidedly aggressive in spite of the Headmaster's statement to the contrary. As the dragon charged it released huge clouds of hissing steam through its nostrils. It was almost as if a gigantic teapot had gone mad. The

dragon came forward so fast and Gawaine was so frightened that he had time to say "Rumplesnitz" only once. As he said it, he swung his battle-ax and off popped the head of the dragon. Gawaine had to admit that it was even easier to kill a real dragon than a wooden one if only you said "Rumplesnitz."

Gawaine brought the ears home and a small section of the tail. His school mates and the faculty made much of him, but the Headmaster wisely kept him from being spoiled by insisting that he go on with his work. Every clear day Gawaine rose at dawn and went out to kill dragons. The Headmaster kept him at home when it rained, because he said the woods were damp and unhealthy at such times and that he didn't want the boy to run needless risks. Few good days passed in which Gawaine failed to get a dragon. On one particularly fortunate day he killed three, a husband and wife and a visiting relative. Gradually he developed a technique. Pupils who sometimes watched him from the hilltops a long way off said that he often allowed the dragon to come within a few feet before he said "Rumplesnitz." He came to say it with a mocking sneer. Occasionally he did stunts. Once when an excursion party from London was watching him he went into action with his right hand tied behind his neck. The dragon's head came off just as easily.

As Gawaine's record of killings mounted higher the Headmaster found it impossible to keep him completely in hand. He fell into the habit of stealing out at night and engaging in long drinking bouts at the village tavern. It was after such a debauch that he rose a little before dawn one fine August morning and started out after his fiftieth dragon. His head was heavy and his mind sluggish. He was heavy in other respects as well, for he had adopted the somewhat vulgar practice of wearing his medals, ribbons and all, when he went out dragon hunting. The decorations began on his chest and ran all the way down to his abdomen. They must have weighed at least eight pounds.

Gawaine found a dragon in the same meadow where he had killed the first one. It was a fair-sized dragon, but evidently an old one. Its face was wrinkled and Gawaine thought he had never seen so hideous a countenance. Much to the lad's disgust, the monster refused to charge and Gawaine was obliged to walk toward him. He whistled as he went. The dragon regarded him hopelessly, but craftily. Of course it had heard of Gawaine. Even when the lad raised his battle-ax the dragon made no move. It knew that there was no salvation in the quickest thrust of the head, for it had been informed that this hunter was protected by an enchantment. It merely waited, hoping something would turn up. Gawaine raised the battle-ax and suddenly lowered it again. He had grown very pale and he trembled violently. The dragon suspected a trick. "What's the matter?" it asked, with false solicitude.

"I've forgotten the magic word," stammered Gawaine.

"What a pity," said the dragon. "So that was the secret. It doesn't seem quite sporting to me, all this magic stuff, you know. Not cricket, as we used to say when I was a little dragon; but after all, that's a matter of opinion."

Gawaine was so helpless with terror that the dragon's confidence rose immeasurably and it could not resist the temptation to show off a bit.

"Could I possibly be of any assistance?" it asked. "What's the first letter of the magic word?"

"It begins with an 'r,'" said Gawaine weakly.

"Let's see," mused the dragon, "that doesn't tell us much, does it? What sort of a word is this? Is it an epithet, do you think?"

Gawaine could do no more than nod.

"Why, of course," exclaimed the dragon, "reactionary Republican."

Gawaine shook his head.

"Well, then," said the dragon, "we'd better get down to business. Will you surrender?"

With the suggestion of a compromise Gawaine mustered up enough courage to speak.

"What will you do if I surrender?" he asked.

"Why, I'll eat you," said the dragon.

"And if I don't surrender?"

"I'll eat you just the same."

"Then it doesn't make any difference, does it?" moaned Gawaine.

"It does to me," said the dragon with a smile. "I'd rather you didn't surrender. You'd taste much better if you didn't."

The dragon waited for a long time for Gawaine to ask "Why?" but the boy was too frightened to speak. At last the dragon had to give the explanation without his cue line. "You see," he said, "if you don't surrender you'll taste better because you'll die game."

This was an old and ancient trick of the dragon's. By means of some such quip he was accustomed to paralyze his victims with laughter and then to destroy them. Gawaine was sufficiently paralyzed as it was, but laughter had no part in his helplessness. With the last word of the joke the dragon drew back his head and struck. In that second there flashed into the mind of Gawaine the magic word "Rumplesnitz," but there was no time to say it. There was time only to strike and, without a word, Gawaine met the onrush of the dragon with a full swing. He put all his back and shoulders into it. The impact was terrific and the head of the dragon flew away almost a hundred yards and landed in a thicket.

Gawaine did not remain frightened very long after the death of the dragon. His mood was one of wonder. He was enormously puzzled. He cut off the ears of the monster almost in a trance. Again and again he thought to himself, "I didn't say 'Rumplesnitz'!" He was sure of that and yet there was no question that he had killed the dragon. In fact, he had never killed one so utterly. Never before had he driven a head for anything like the same distance. Twenty-five yards was perhaps his best previous record. All the way back to the knight school he kept rumbling about in his mind seeking an explanation for what had occurred. He went to the Headmaster immediately and after closing the door told him what had happened. "I didn't say 'Rumplesnitz,'" he explained with great earnestness.

The Headmaster laughed. "I'm glad you've found out," he said. "It makes you ever so much more of a hero. Don't you see that? Now you know that it was you who killed all these dragons and not that foolish little word 'Rumplesnitz.'"

Gawaine frowned. "Then it wasn't a magic word after all?" he asked.

"Of course not," said the Headmaster. "You ought to be too old for such foolishness. There isn't any such thing as a magic word."

"But you told me it was magic," protested Gawaine. "You said it was magic and now you say it isn't."

"It wasn't magic in a literal sense," answered the Headmaster, "but it was much more wonderful than that. The word gave you confidence. It took away fears. If I hadn't told you that you might have been killed the very first time. It was your battle-ax did the trick."

Gawaine surprised the Headmaster by his attitude. He was obviously distressed by the explanation. He interrupted a long philosophic and ethical discourse by the Headmaster with, "If I hadn't of hit 'em all mighty hard and fast any one of 'em might have crushed me like a, like a—" He fumbled for a word.

"Egg shell," suggested the Headmaster.

"Like a egg shell," assented Gawaine, and he said it many times. All through the evening meal people who sat near him heard him muttering. "Like a egg shell, like a egg shell."

The next day was clear, but Gawaine did not get up at dawn. Indeed, it was almost noon when the Headmaster found him cowering in bed, with the clothes pulled over his head. The principal called the Assistant Professor of Pleasaunce, and together they dragged the boy toward the forest.

"He'll be all right as soon as he gets a couple more dragons under his belt," explained the Headmaster.

The Assistant Professor of Pleasaunce agreed. "It would be a shame to stop such a fine run," he said. "Why, counting that one yesterday, he's killed fifty dragons."

They pushed the boy into a thicket above which hung a meager cloud of steam. It was obviously quite a small dragon. But Gawaine did not come back that night or the next. In fact, he never came back. Some weeks afterward brave spirits from the school explored the thicket, but they could find nothing to remind them of Gawaine except the metal parts of his medals. Even the ribbons had been devoured.

The Headmaster and the Assistant Professor of Pleasaunce agreed that it would be just as well not to tell the school how Gawaine had achieved his record and still less how he came to die. They held that it might have a bad effect on school spirit. Accordingly, Gawaine has lived in the memory of the school as its greatest hero. No visitor succeeds in leaving the building today without seeing a great shield which hangs on the wall of the dining hall. Fifty pairs of dragons' ears are mounted upon the shield and underneath in gilt letters is "Gawaine Le Coeur-Hardy," followed by the simple inscription, "He killed fifty dragons." The record has never been equaled.

# The STORY of CHICKEN Little

*by Walt Kelly*

One day Chicken Little was standing by his own self out in the woods and a-mindin' of his own business.

What you doin' out here, son?
Like it say in the story, I is mindin' my own business.
Smart li'l' sprat!
plunk!
Ooh!

From *Uncle Pogo So-So Stories.*

Somethin' is fell an' knock my hat over my baby blue eyes!
A piece of sky.
The sky is fallin'!
Run off, Chicken Little, chile, and bear them tidings to the king!
Henny-Penny! Henny-Penny! We gotta go see the King!
How come, Chicken Li'l'?
SCRATCH SHEET
'Cause the sky is fallin'! It already knock my hat overn my eyeballs as you kin see!
Proof fo' sho' nuff!
There I was, mindin' my own business hand over foots, an' all over sudden a big hunk of sky clunk down on my head bone an'---

Oh, Owly-Jowly! The sky is a-fallin' an' us gotta git over to the King's palace!
It was me got hit, sir, right on the head.
Sho' nuff?
I'm the one got hit, Owly-Powly! Me an' Henny-Penny is sharin' the gossip, so to speak.
Isn't it awful? The sky fell an' hit me right on the hat! Well, sir! You can imagine---
Turtle-Lurtle! Chicken Little, Owly-Jowly an' me, Henny-Penny, is runnin' to tell the King the sky is fallin'.
Truly ruly?
I felt that this was indeed a moment for courage, so I---
Hats off to you!
Oh, I agreely really!
On-on-on-on-on-on---
I immediately contacted Henny-Penny and she said to me, she said, "Chicken Little," she said--- hey, its gettin' dark!

What's all the fuss, Henny-Penny?
Chicken Little, Owly-Mowly, Turtle-Wurtle, an' Henny Penny is runnin' to tell the King that the sky is fallin'.
May I go with you, Chicken Little, Owly-Dowly, Turtle-Wurtle an' Henny-Penny?
Yes, indeed, Doggy-Soggy.
Why call me Doggy-Soggy? Why not Doggy-Loggy or Doggy-Toggy or somethin'?
I was the one what discovered the sky was fallin', sir. I used my head an'---
On to the King---on on on on on on on on!
What?
I was sayin' it was me saw the sky was fallin', Doggy-Foggy--- I very alertly contacted Henny-Penny. "Henny," I said, "do you know the skyey-wyey is fallin'?" Well, ha! You should of---
Beaver smeaver! Beaver smeaver! Beaver smeaver!

Doggy-Smoggy, Owly-Rowly, Turkle-Murkle, Henny-Penny an' Chicken Little is gone tell the King the sky is fallin'.
May I go with you, Owly-Howly, Turtle-Hurtle, Henny-Penny and---uh-uh---who else?
Me, Doggy-Doggy!
An'me, Chicken Little, who is the famous discoverer of the fallin' sky---I was out in the woods, mind you, mindin' my own business when all at once a big piece of the sky fell on---
Naturally I looked up Henny-Penny and told her. She said, "Chicken Little, we better run off," she said, "an' tell the King," she said. Well! So I up an'---
Hoo, boy--- Froggy-Groggy! Froggy-Groggy!

Owly Cowly, Turtle Squirtle, Doggle-Boggle, Beaver-Smeaver, Chicken Little an' Henny-Penny are going to tell the King the sky is fallin'.
You hear, Froggy-Groggy?
Rowr!
Snap! Snap!
I'm a Toady-Loady! Not a Froggy-Smoggy!
I'll tell the King on you! You snapped at me!
Come along, Toady-Loady. I'll get you a front position when we see the King because I happen to be the one on who the sky fell on. A big piece hit me on the hat and I, quick as a flash, I said, "Hey," I said, "the sky---"

He comin'! He comin'!
Rowf! Rowf! Rowf!
Oh, Ducky-Wucky! Toady-Loady, Chicken Little, Beaver-Smeaver, Doggy-Groggy, Owly-Jowly, Turtle-Purtle and me, Henny-Penny, is runnin' to tell the King the sky is fallin'!
It's a good day for a li'l' run, Ducky-Wucky.
You call me Ducky-Wucky again and I'll poke you on the nosey-posey!
Oh, Foxy-Loxy! Toady-Loady, Chicken Little, Beaver-Smeaver, Doggy-Groggy, Owl-Wowl, Turtle Snurtle, Ducky-Stucky an' Henny-Penny is runnin' to tell the King the sky is fallin'.
Well, Toady-Loady, Chicken-Little, Beaver-Steaver, Doggy-Foggy, Owly-Sowly, Turtle-Purple, Ducky-Clucky, Henny Penny! I know where the King lives---a deep, dark cave---I'll lead you to it!
Oh, thank you, Foxy-Moxy!

Oh, Pogo-Logo! We all is a-runnin' to tell the King the sky is a-fallin'!
An' I knows where the King lives!
What king?
Yeah, what king?
Yeah, what?
Yeah!
Yeah, what king?
What king indeed?
Oh, yes--- the King? Well--uh--- you know, the King.
Phoo!
SEE THE KING 5¢
Yoo hoo!
Oh boy! There's the King! The King!
Phoo Phoo!

Put the money in the box, friends! Step lively an' no crowding. Immediate seating!
SEE THE KING 5¢
My sakes---any of you folks happen to got the borry of a five cent piece?
Not me.
Nor me.
Not me.
Not me.
Nor me.
I been keepin' my wealth under my hat. Happen I do got a whole nickel coin.
Dog my cats!
So I gits to see the King!
Gosh!
Step right in, folks---don't push, please---take it easy. No need for jamming the aisles.
CLINK

Thunk they was a multitude gone see the King?
I is it.
Dog bone! You isn't much of a multitude.
I is the best we got, an' besides, I knows the whole story.
Hey! I been tryin' to catch up! That wasn't the sky what fell! It was a acorn!
Don't be ridiculous!
Would we be takin' up the King's time about a acorn?
There I was, see, and this hunk of sky fell right on my hat---well, sir---
SEE THE KING 5¢
The sky ain't really fallin', Pogo. Don't worry---ain't nothin' to tell the King about.
I know--- ain't even no king.
Isolationist!
Yeah!
I run an' tole Henny-Penny, an' she said, "Chicken Little," she said, "the sky is a-fallin'," she said, "an' if we---
If you gone do more talkin', put another nickel in.

# The Little Girl and the Wolf

*by James Thurber*

*James Thurber grew up to be one of America's greatest and most popular humorists. (His superb story, "The Night the Bed Fell," is reprinted in this volume.) But when he was a little boy there was one nursery tale that invariably scared the daylights out of him. That was the account of Little Red Riding Hood's trouble with the Big, Bad Wolf. So just as soon as Mr. Thurber grew up he wrote his* own *version of the affair—and here it is.*—B.C.

One afternoon a big wolf waited in a dark forest for a little girl to come along carrying a basket of food for her grandmother. Finally a little girl did come along and she was carrying a basket of food.

From *The New Yorker*.

"Are you carrying that basket to your grandmother?" asked the wolf. The little girl said, yes, she was. So the wolf asked her where her grandmother lived and the little girl told him and he disappeared into the woods.

When the little girl opened the door of her grandmother's house she saw that there was somebody in bed with a nightcap and nightgown on. She had approached no nearer than twenty-five feet from the bed when she saw that it was not her grandmother but the wolf, for even in a nightcap a wolf does not look any more like your grandmother than the Metro-Goldwyn-Mayer lion looks like Calvin Coolidge. So the little girl took an automatic out of her basket and shot the wolf dead.

MORAL: IT IS NOT SO EASY TO FOOL LITTLE GIRLS NOWADAYS AS IT USED TO BE.

# The Ransom of Red Chief

*by O. Henry*

It looked like a good thing: but wait till I tell you. We were down South, in Alabama—Bill Driscoll and myself—when this kidnapping idea struck us. It was, as Bill afterward expressed it, "during a moment of temporary mental apparition"; but we didn't find that out till later.

There was a town down there, as flat as a flannel-cake, and called Summit, of course. It contained inhabitants of as undeleterious and self-satisfied a class of peasantry as ever clustered around a Maypole.

Bill and me had a joint capital of about six hundred dollars, and we needed just two thousand dollars more to pull off a fraudulent town-lot scheme in Western Illinois with. We talked it over on the front steps of the Hotel. Philoprogenitiveness, says we, is strong in semi-rural communities; therefore, and for other reasons, a kidnapping project ought to do better there than in the radius of newspapers that send reporters out in plain clothes to stir up talk about such things. We knew that Summit couldn't get after us with anything stronger than constables and, maybe, some lackadaisical bloodhounds and a diatribe or two in the *Weekly Farmers' Budget*. So, it looked good.

We selected for our victim the only child of a prominent citizen named Ebenezer Dorset. The father was respectable and tight, a mortgage fancier and a stern, upright collection-plate passer and forecloser. The kid was a boy of ten, with bas-relief freckles, and hair the color of the cover of the magazine you buy at the news-

---

From *Whirligigs*.

stand when you want to catch a train. Bill and me figured that Ebenezer would melt down for a ransom of two thousand dollars to a cent. But wait till I tell you.

About two miles from Summit was a little mountain, covered with a dense cedar brake. On the rear elevation of this mountain was a cave. There we stored provisions.

One evening after sundown, we drove in a buggy past old Dorset's house. The kid was in the street, throwing rocks at a kitten on the opposite fence.

"Hey, little boy!" says Bill, "would you like to have a bag of candy and a nice ride?"

The boy catches Bill neatly in the eye with a piece of brick.

"That will cost the old man an extra five hundred dollars," says Bill, climbing over the wheel.

That boy put up a fight like a welter-weight cinnamon bear; but, at last, we got him down in the bottom of the buggy and drove away. We took him up to the cave, and I hitched the horse in the cedar brake. After dark I drove the buggy to the little village, three miles away, where we had hired it, and walked back to the mountain.

Bill was pasting court-plaster over the scratches and bruises on his features. There was a fire burning behind the big rock at the entrance of the cave, and the boy was watching a pot of boiling coffee, with two buzzard tail-feathers stuck in his red hair. He points a stick at me when I come up, and says:

"Ha! cursed paleface, do you dare to enter the camp of Red Chief, the terror of the plains?"

"He's all right now," says Bill, rolling up his trousers and examining some bruises on his shins. "We're playing Indian. We're making Buffalo Bill's show look like magic-lantern views of Palestine in the town hall. I'm Old Hank, the Trapper, Red Chief's captive, and I'm to be scalped at daybreak. By Geronimo! that kid can kick hard."

Yes, sir, that boy seemed to be having the time of his life. The fun of camping out in a cave had made him forget that he was a captive himself. He immediately christened me Snake-eye, the Spy, and announced that, when his braves returned from the warpath, I was to be broiled at the stake at the rising of the sun.

Then we had supper; and he filled his mouth full of bacon and bread and gravy, and began to talk. He made a during-dinner speech something like this:

"I like this fine. I never camped out before; but I had a pet 'possum once, and I was nine last birthday. I hate to go to school. Rats ate up sixteen of Jimmy Talbot's aunt's speckled hen's eggs. Are there any real Indians in these woods? I want some more gravy. Does the trees moving make the wind blow? We had five puppies. What makes your nose so red, Hank? My father has lots of money. Are the stars hot? I whipped Ed Walker twice, Saturday. I don't like girls. You dassent catch toads unless with a string. Do oxen make any noise? Why are oranges round? Have you got beds to sleep on in this cave? Amos Murray has got six toes. A parrot can talk, but a monkey or a fish can't. How many does it take to make twelve?"

Every few minutes he would remember that he was a pesky redskin, and pick up his stick rifle and tiptoe to the mouth of the cave to rubber for the scouts of the hated paleface. Now and then he would let out a war-whoop that made Old Hank the Trapper shiver. That boy had Bill terrorized from the start.

"Red Chief," says I to the kid, "would you like to go home?"

"Aw, what for?" says he. "I don't have any fun at home. I hate to go to school. I like to camp out. You won't take me back home again, Snake-eye, will you?"

"Not right away," says I. "We'll stay here in the cave awhile."

"All right!" says he. "That'll be fine. I never had such fun in all my life."

We went to bed about eleven o'clock. We spread down some wide blankets and quilts and put Red Chief between us. We weren't afraid he'd run away. He kept us awake for three hours, jumping up and reaching for his rifle and screeching: "Hist! pard," in mine and Bill's ears, as the fancied crackle of a twig or the rustle of a leaf revealed to his young imagination the stealthy approach of the outlaw band. At last, I fell into a troubled sleep, and dreamed that I had been kidnapped and chained to a tree by a ferocious pirate with red hair.

Just at daybreak, I was awakened by a series of awful screams from Bill. They weren't yells, or howls, or shouts, or whoops, or yawps, such as you'd expect from a manly set of vocal organs—they were simply indecent, terrifying, humiliating screams, such as women emit when they see ghosts or caterpillars. It's an awful thing to hear a strong, desperate, fat man scream incontinently in a cave at daybreak.

I jumped up to see what the matter was. Red Chief was sitting on Bill's chest, with one hand twined in Bill's hair. In the other he had the sharp case-knife we used for slicing bacon; and he was industriously and realistically trying to take Bill's scalp, according to the sentence that had been pronounced upon him the evening before.

I got the knife away from the kid and made him lie down again. But, from that moment, Bill's spirit was broken. He laid down on his side of the bed, but he never closed an eye again in sleep as long as that boy was with us. I dozed off for a while, but along toward sun-up I remembered that Red Chief had said I was to be burned at the stake at the rising of the sun. I wasn't nervous or afraid; but I sat up and lit my pipe and leaned against a rock.

"What you getting up so soon for, Sam?" asked Bill.

"Me?" says I. "Oh, I got a kind of pain in my shoulder. I thought sitting up would rest it."

"You're a liar!" says Bill. "You're afraid. You was to be burned at sunrise, and you was afraid he'd do it. And he would, too, if he could find a match. Ain't it awful, Sam? Do you think anybody will pay out money to get a little imp like that back home?"

"Sure," said I. "A rowdy kid like that is just the kind that parents dote on. Now, you and the Chief get up and cook breakfast, while I go up on the top of this mountain and reconnoitre."

I went up on the peak of the little mountain and ran my eye over the contiguous vicinity. Over towards Summit I expected to see the sturdy yeomanry of the village armed with scythes and pitchforks beating the countryside for the dastardly kidnappers. But what I saw was a peaceful landscape dotted with one man ploughing with a dun mule. Nobody was dragging the creek; no couriers dashed hither and yon, bringing tidings of no news to the distracted parents. There was a sylvan attitude of somnolent sleepiness pervading that section of the external outward surface of Alabama that lay exposed to my view. "Perhaps," says I to myself, "it has not yet been discovered that the wolves have borne away the tender lambkin from the fold. Heaven help the wolves!" says I, and I went down the mountain to breakfast.

When I got to the cave I found Bill backed up against the side of it, breathing hard, and the boy threatening to smash him with a rock half as big as a cocoanut.

"He put a red-hot boiled potato down my back," explained Bill, "and then mashed it with his foot; and I boxed his ears. Have you got a gun about you, Sam?"

I took the rock away from the boy and kind of patched up the argument. "I'll fix you," says the kid to Bill. "No man ever yet struck the Red Chief but he got paid for it. You better beware!"

After breakfast the kid takes a piece of leather with strings wrapped around it out of his pocket and goes outside the cave unwinding it.

"What's he up to now?" says Bill, anxiously. "You don't think he'll run away, do you, Sam?"

"No fear of it," says I. "He don't seem to be much of a home body. But we've got to fix up some plan about the ransom. There don't seem to be much excitement around Summit on account of his disappearance; but maybe they haven't realized yet that he's gone. His folks may think he's spending the night with Aunt Jane or one of the neighbors. Anyhow, he'll be missed today. Tonight we must get a message to his father demanding the two thousand dollars for his return."

Just then we heard a kind of war-whoop, such as David might have emitted when he knocked out the champion Goliath. It was a sling that Red Chief had pulled out of his pocket, and he was whirling it around his head.

I dodged, and heard a heavy thud and a kind of a sigh from Bill, like a horse gives out when you take his saddle off. A rock the size of an egg had caught Bill just behind his left ear. He loosened himself all over and fell in the fire across the frying pan of hot water for washing the dishes. I dragged him out and poured cold water on his head for half an hour.

By and by, Bill sits up and feels behind his ear and says: "Sam, do you know who my favorite Biblical character is?"

"Take it easy," says I. "You'll come to your senses presently."

"King Herod," says he. "You won't go away and leave me here alone, will you, Sam?"

I went out and caught that boy and shook him until his freckles rattled.

"If you don't behave," says I, "I'll take you straight home. Now, are you going to be good, or not?"

"I was only funning," says he, sullenly, "I didn't mean to hurt Old Hank. But what did he hit me for? I'll behave, Snake-eye, if you won't send me home, and if you'll let me play the Black Scout today."

"I don't know the game," says I. "That's for you and Mr. Bill to decide. He's your playmate for the day. I'm going away for a while, on business. Now, you come in and make friends with him and say you are sorry for hurting him, or home you go, at once."

I made him and Bill shake hands, and then I took Bill aside and told him I was going to Poplar Grove, a little village three miles from the cave, and find out what I could about how the kidnapping had been regarded in Summit. Also, I thought it best to send a peremptory letter to old man Dorset that day, demanding the ransom and dictating how it should be paid.

"You know, Sam," says Bill, "I've stood by you without batting an eye in earthquakes, fire and flood—in poker games, dynamite outrages, police raids, train robberies, and cyclones. I never lost my nerve yet till we kidnapped that two-legged skyrocket of a kid. He's got me going. You won't leave me long with him, will you, Sam?"

"I'll be back some time this afternoon," says I. "You must keep the boy amused and quiet till I return. And now we'll write the letter to old Dorset."

Bill and I got paper and pencil and worked on the letter while Red Chief, with a blanket wrapped around him, strutted up and down, guarding the mouth of the cave. Bill begged me tearfully to make the ransom fifteen hundred dollars instead of two thousand. "I ain't attempting," says he, "to decry the celebrated moral aspect of parental affection, but we're dealing with humans, and it ain't human for anybody to give up two thousand dollars for that forty-pound chunk of freckled wildcat. I'm willing to take a chance at fifteen hundred dollars. You can charge the difference up to me."

So, to relieve Bill, I acceded, and we collaborated a letter that ran this way:

Ebenezer Dorset, Esq.:

We have your boy concealed in a place far from Summit. It is useless for you or the most skillful detectives to attempt to find him. Absolutely, the only terms on which you can have him restored to you are these: We demand fifteen hundred dollars in large bills for his return; the money to be left at midnight tonight at the same spot and in the same box as your reply—as hereinafter described. If you agree to these terms, send your answer in writing by a solitary messenger tonight at half-past eight o'clock. After crossing Owl Creek on the road to Poplar Grove, there are three large trees about a hundred yards apart, close to the fence of the wheat field on the right-hand side. At the bottom of the fence-post, opposite the third tree, will be found a small pasteboard box.

The messenger will place the answer in this box and return immediately to Summit.

If you attempt any treachery or fail to comply with our demand as stated, you will never see your boy again.

If you pay the money as demanded, he will be returned to you safe and well within three hours. These terms are final, and if you do not accede to them no further communication will be attempted.

TWO DESPERATE MEN

I addressed this letter to Dorset, and put it in my pocket. As I was about to start, the kid comes up to me and says:

"Aw, Snake-eye, you said I could play the Black Scout while you was gone."

"Play it, of course," says I. "Mr. Bill will play with you. What kind of a game is it?"

"I'm the Black Scout," says Red Chief, "and I have to ride to the stockade to warn the settlers that the Indians are coming. I'm tired of playing Indian myself. I want to be the Black Scout."

"All right," says I. "It sounds harmless to me. I guess Mr. Bill will help you foil the pesky savages."

"What am I to do?" asks Bill, looking at the kid suspiciously.

"You are the hoss," says Black Scout. "Get down on your hands and knees. How can I ride to the stockade without a hoss?"

"You'd better keep him interested," said I, "till we get the scheme going. Loosen up."

Bill gets down on his all fours, and a look comes in his eye like a rabbit's when you catch it in a trap.

"How far is it to the stockade, kid?" he asks, in a husky manner of voice.

"Ninety miles," says the Black Scout. "And you have to hump yourself to get there on time. Whoa, now!"

The Black Scout jumps on Bill's back and digs his heels in his side.

"For Heaven's sake," says Bill, "hurry back, Sam, as soon as you can. I wish we hadn't made the ransom more than a thousand. Say, you quit kicking me or I'll get up and warm you good."

I walked over to Poplar Grove and sat around the post office and store, talking with the chaw-bacons that came in to trade. One whiskerando says that he hears Summit is all upset on account of Elder Ebenezer Dorset's boy having been lost or stolen. That was all I wanted to know. I bought some smoking tobacco, referred casually to the price of black-eyed peas, posted my letter surreptitiously, and came away. The postmaster said the mail-carrier would come by in an hour to take the mail to Summit.

When I got back to the cave Bill and the boy were not to be found. I explored the vicinity of the cave, and risked a yodel or two, but there was no response.

So I lighted my pipe and sat down on a mossy bank to await developments.

In about half an hour I heard the bushes rustle, and Bill wabbled out into the little glade in front of the cave. Behind him was the kid, stepping softly like a scout, with a broad grin on his face. Bill stopped, took off his hat, and wiped his face with a red handkerchief. The kid stopped about eight feet behind him.

"Sam," says Bill, "I suppose you'll think I'm a renegade, but I couldn't help it. I'm a grown person with masculine proclivities and habits of self-defense, but there is a time when all systems of egotism and predominance fail. The boy is gone. I sent him home.

All is off. There was martyrs in old times," goes on Bill, "that suffered death rather than give up the particular graft they enjoyed. None of 'em ever was subjugated to such supernatural tortures as I have been. I tried to be faithful to our articles of depredation; but there came a limit."

"What's the trouble, Bill?" I asks him.

"I was rode," says Bill, "the ninety miles to the stockade, not barring an inch. Then, when the settlers was rescued, I was given oats. Sand ain't a palatable substitute. And then, for an hour I had to try to explain to him why there was nothin' in holes, how a road can run both ways, and what makes the grass green. I tell you, Sam, a human can only stand so much. I takes him by the neck of his clothes and drags him down the mountain. On the way he kicks my legs black and blue from the knees down; and I've got to have two or three bites on my thumb and hand cauterized.

"But he's gone"—continues Bill—"gone home. I showed him the road to Summit and kicked him about eight feet nearer there at one kick. I'm sorry we lose the ransom; but it was either that or Bill Driscoll to the madhouse."

Bill is puffing and blowing, but there is a look of ineffable peace and growing content on his rose-pink features.

"Bill," says I, "there isn't any heart disease in your family, is there?"

"No," says Bill, "nothing chronic except malaria and accidents. Why?"

"Then you might turn around," says I, "and have a look behind you."

Bill turns and sees the boy, and loses his complexion and sits down plump on the ground and begins to pluck aimlessly at grass and little sticks. For an hour I was afraid of his mind. And then I told him that my scheme was to put the whole job through immediately and that we would get the ransom and be off with it by midnight if old Dorset fell in with our proposition. So Bill braced up enough to give the kid a weak sort of a smile and a promise to play the Russian in a Japanese war with him as soon as he felt a little better.

I had a scheme for collecting that ransom without danger of being caught by counterplots that ought to commend itself to professional kidnappers. The tree under which the answer was to be left—and the money later on—was close to the road fence with

big, bare fields on all sides. If a gang of constables should be watching for anyone to come for the note, they could see him a long way off crossing the fields or in the road. But no, sirree! At half-past eight I was up in that tree as well hidden as a tree toad, waiting for the messenger to arrive.

Exactly on time, a half-grown boy rides up the road on a bicycle, locates the pasteboard box at the foot of the fencepost, slips a folded piece of paper into it, and pedals away again back toward Summit.

I waited an hour and then concluded the thing was square. I

slid down the tree, got the note, slipped along the fence till I struck the woods, and was back at the cave in another half an hour. I opened the note, got near the lantern, and read it to Bill. It was written with a pen in a crabbed hand, and the sum and substance of it was this:

> Two Desperate Men.
>
> *Gentlemen:* I received your letter today by post, in regard to the ransom you ask for the return of my son. I think you are a little high in your demands, and I hereby make you a counterproposition, which I am inclined to believe you will accept. You bring Johnny home and pay me two hundred and fifty dollars in cash, and I agree to take him off your hands. You had better come at night, for the neighbors believe he is lost, and I couldn't be responsible for what they would do to anybody they saw bringing him back. Very respectfully,
>
> EBENEZER DORSET

"Great Pirates of Penzance," says I; "of all the impudent—"

But I glanced at Bill, and hesitated. He had the most appealing look in his eyes I ever saw on the face of a dumb or a talking brute.

"Sam," says he, "what's two hundred and fifty dollars, after all? We've got the money. One more night of this kid will send me to a bed in Bedlam. Besides being a thorough gentleman, I think Mr. Dorset is a spendthrift for making us such a liberal offer. You ain't going to let the chance go, are you?"

"Tell you the truth, Bill," says I, "this little he ewe lamb has somewhat got on my nerves too. We'll take him home, pay the ransom, and make our getaway."

We took him home that night. We got him to go by telling him that his father had bought a silver-mounted rifle and a pair of moccasins for him, and we were to hunt bears the next day.

It was just twelve o'clock when we knocked at Ebenezer's front door. Just at the moment when I should have been abstracting the fifteen hundred dollars from the box under the tree, according to the original proposition, Bill was counting out two hundred and fifty dollars into Dorset's hand.

When the kid found out we were going to leave him at home he started up a howl like a calliope and fastened himself as tight as a leech to Bill's leg. His father peeled him away gradually, like a porous plaster.

"How long can you hold him?" asks Bill.

"I'm not as strong as I used to be," says old Dorset. "But I think I can promise you ten minutes."

"Enough," says Bill. "In ten minutes I shall cross the Central, Southern, and Middle Western States, and be legging it trippingly for the Canadian border."

And, as dark as it was, and as fat as Bill was, and as good a runner as I am, he was a good mile and a half out of Summit before I could catch up with him.

# Riddle-de-Dee

*Collected by Bennett Cerf*

Q. What did the duck say when it laid a square egg?
A. "Ouch!"

Q. Why is a pig's tail like getting up at 4:40 A.M.?
A. It's twirly.

Q. What's black and white and red all over?
A. A blushing zebra.

Q. When do giraffes have eight legs?
A. When there are two of them.

Q. A man fell out of a tenth-story window but was barely scratched. Why?
A. He was wearing a light fall suit.

Q. Four men fell into the water, but only three of them got their hair wet. Why?
A. One of them was bald.

Q. What are the three most common causes of forest fires?
A. Men, women, and children.

Q. How can you divide sixteen apples among seventeen hungry people?
A. Make applesauce.

Q. What time is it when the clock strikes thirteen?
A. Time to get the clock fixed.

---

From the book *Riddle-de-Dee*.

Q. How can you tell a male hippopotamus from a female hippopotamus?
A. Ask it a question. If *he* answers, it's a male; if *she* answers, it's a female.

Q. Why do they have mirrors on chewing-gum machines?
A. So you can see how you look when the gum doesn't come out.

Q. Which is bigger: Mr. Bigger or Mr. Bigger's baby?
A. The baby is a little Bigger.

Q. How can you stop a small child from spilling food at the table?
A. Feed him on the floor.

Q. When should a boy kick about something he gets for his birthday?
A. When he gets a football.

Q. Why did a mother knit her G.I. son three socks?
A. Because he wrote that he had grown another foot.

Q. Who has the most friends for lunch?
A. A cannibal.

Q. What's worse than finding a worm in an apple?
A. Finding half a worm.

Q. When should a baker quit making doughnuts?
A. When he gets sick of the hole business.

Q. What's the best way to keep milk from turning sour?
A. Keep it inside the cow.

Q. Name a product raised in countries where there's lots of rain.
A. Umbrellas.

Q. What has four legs and one foot?
A. A bed.

Q. What was the largest island in the world before Australia was discovered?
A. Australia.

Q. Is it harmful to write on an empty stomach?
A. No, but paper is better.

Q. How can you live to be one hundred years old?
A. Drink a glass of milk every morning for twelve hundred months.

Q. Why is a traffic cop the strongest man in the world?
A. Because he can hold up a ten-ton truck with one hand.

Q. What has eighteen legs and catches flies?
A. A baseball team.

Q. What contains more feet in winter than in summer?
A. A skating rink.

Q. Why did Robin Hood rob only the rich?
A. Because the poor had no money.

Q. Why is it useless to send a letter to Washington?
A. Because he died in 1799.

Q. Where was the Declaration of Independence signed?
A. At the bottom.

Q. What did the big toe say to the little toe?
A. "Don't look now, but there's a heel following us."

Q. Which is faster: heat or cold?
A. Heat. You can catch cold.

Q. What animal drops from the clouds?
A. The rain, dear.

Q. What question can *never* be answered "Yes"?
A. "Are you asleep?"

Q. What question must *always* be answered "Yes"?
A. "What does Y-E-S spell?"

Q. What word is always pronounced wrong?
A. Wrong.

Q. What did the rake say to the hoe?
A. Hi, hoe!

Q. How can you find a rabbit that is lost in the woods?
A. Make a noise like a carrot.

Q. Why do humming birds hum?
A. Because they don't know the words.

# How Beautiful with Mud

*by Hildegarde Dolson*

Perhaps the surest way to tell when a female goes over the boundary from childhood into meaningful adolescence is to watch how long it takes her to get to bed at night. My own cross-over, which could be summed up in our family as "What on earth is Hildegarde *doing* in the bathroom?" must have occurred when I was a freshman in high school. Until then, I fell into bed dog-tired each night, after the briefest possible bout with toothbrush and washcloth. But once I'd become aware of the Body Beautiful, as portrayed in advertisements in women's magazines, my absorption was complete and my attitude highly optimistic. I too would be beautiful. I would also be Flower-Fresh, Fastidious and Dainty—a triple-threat virtue obviously prized above pearls by the entire male sex, as depicted in the *Ladies' Home Journal.*

Somehow, out of my dollar-a-week allowance, I managed to buy Mum, Odorono, Listerine and something called Nipso, the latter guaranteed to remove excess hair from arms and legs, and make a man think, "Oooo, what a flawless surface." It's true that I had no men, nor was I a particularly hairy child, having only a light yellow down on my angular appendages. Nevertheless, I applied the Nipso painstakingly in the bathroom one night with Sally as my interested audience. I had noticed the stuff had a rather overpowering, sickish sweet scent, but this was a very minor drawback, considering the goal I had in mind. After Sally had been watching me for a few minutes, she began holding her nose. Finally she asked me to unlock the door and let her out. "Don't you want to see me wash it

---

From *We Shook the Family Tree.*

off?" I asked, rather hurt.

"No," Sally said. "It smells funny."

In the next hour, as my father, mother and brothers followed their noses to the upstairs hall, there were far more detailed descriptions of just how Nipso affected the olfactory senses. Jimmy, being a simple child, merely said "Pugh" and went away. My father thought it was most like the odor of rotten eggs, but Bobby said No, it was more like a mouse that's been dead quite a while. Mother was more tactful, only remarking that Nipso obviously wasn't meant to be applied in a house people lived in. Since it certainly wasn't meant to be applied in a wooded dell, either, I was prevailed upon to throw the rest of the tube away.

I didn't mind too much, because I already had my eye on something that sounded far more fascinating than Nipso. This was a miraculous substance called Beauty Clay, and every time I read about it in a magazine advertisement, the words enveloped me in rapture. Even the story of its discovery was a masterpiece in lyrical prose. Seems this girl was traveling in an obscure European country (name on request) and ran out of those things ladies always run out of at the wrong time, such as powder and make-up lotion. The worse part was that the girl really *needed* such artifices to cover up bumps. Through some intuitive process which escapes me at the moment, she had the presence of mind to go to a near-by hamlet, pick up a handful of mud, and plaster it on her face. Then she lay dozing in the sun, by a brook. When she came to, washed the claylike mud off her face, and looked at her reflection in the brook, she knew she had hit the jackpot. Boy, she was beautiful. Looking at the Before-and-After pictures, I could see that *this* beauty was more than skin-deep, having benefited even her nose, eyes and hair.

After pondering all this, I could well understand why a jar of the imported Beauty Clay cost $4.98. In fact, it was dirt cheap at the price, and my only problem was how to lay my hands on $4.98. Certainly I had no intention of enlisting financial support from my parents. For one thing, it was too much money, and for another thing, parents ask too many questions. Far better, I thought, to let the transformation of their oldest daughter come as a dazzling surprise.

Due to the fact that I had such important things as Beauty Clay on my mind, it was understandable that my monthly marks in algebra should cause even more distress than usual in the bosom of my family. Each month, the high-school honor roll, consisting of the names of the ten highest students in each class, was published in the *Franklin News-Herald.* And each month, my own name was prominently absent. Appeals to my better nature, my pride, and the honor of the Dolsons did no good. I honestly meant well, and I even went so far as to carry books home from school and carry them back again the next morning. But freshman algebra, implying as it did that X equals Y, was simply beyond me. Finally my father said that if I got on the Honor Roll he'd give me five dollars. Wobbly as I was in mathematics, it took me only a flash to realize this sum was approximately equal to $4.98, or the piddling price of the Beauty Clay. From there on in, I was straining every muscle. When I say that I got 89 in algebra and climbed to the bottom rung of the Honor Roll, I am stating a miracle simply. What is more important, I got the five bucks.

My father said that if I liked, he'd put most of it in my savings account. Bobby said, with even more enthusiasm, that he knew where I could get a bargain in a second-hand pistol. I declined both offers, marveling at the things men could think of to do with money, and made my way, on foot, to Riesenman's drugstore. When Mr. Riesenman said he had no Beauty Clay, I was grieved. When he said he'd never even heard of the stuff, I was appalled. It took three trips to convince him that he must order it immediately, money on the line.

Then I went home and waited. With admirable restraint, I waited five days. After that, I made daily inquiries on my way home from school. If I was with friends, I'd say I had to do an errand for Mother and would catch up to them later. They must often have wondered, in the next thirty days, at the number of unobtainable items my mother demanded of a drugstore. Finally came the wonderful afternoon when Mr. Riesenman said, "Here you are, Hildegarde." His jovial air may have been due to the fact that he was rid of me at last. My own joy was primitive and unconfined. At last I'd got hold of a rainbow.

It took a week more before I could achieve the needed privacy for my quick-change act. Mother was taking Jimmy and Sally downtown to get new shoes, Bobby was going skiing, and my father, as usual, would be at the office. I got home to the empty house at twenty minutes of four, and made a beeline for the Beauty Clay. According to the directions, I then washed off all make-up, which in my own case was a faint dash of powder on my nose, and wrapped myself in a sheet "To protect that pretty frock," or, more accurately, my blue-serge middy blouse. Then I took a small wooden spatula the manufacturer had thoughtfully provided, and dug into the jar.

The Beauty Clay was a rather peculiar shade of grayish-green, and I spread this all over my face and neck—"even to the hairline where tell-tale wrinkles hide." The directions also urged me not to talk or smile during the twenty minutes it would take the clay to dry. The last thing in the world I wanted to do was talk or smile. That could come later. For now, a reverent silence would suffice. In fact, as the thick green clay dried firmly in place, it had to suffice. Even though my face and neck felt as if they'd been cast in cement, the very sensation reassured me. Obviously, something was happening. I sat bolt upright in a chair and let it happen.

After fifteen minutes of this, the doorbell rang. I decided to ignore it. The doorbell rang again and again, jangling at my conscience. Nobody at our house ever ignored doorbells, and I was relieved when it stopped. In my eagerness to see who had been calling on us, I ran to my window, opened it, and leaned out. The departing guest was only the man who brought us country butter each week, I was glad to note. Hearing the sound of the window opening above him, he looked up. When he saw me leaning out, his mouth dropped open and he let out a hoarse, awful sound. Then he turned and ran down the steep hill at incredible speed. I couldn't imagine what had struck him, to act so foolish.

It wasn't until I'd remembered the clay and went to look in a mirror that I understood. Swathed in a sheet, and with every visible millimeter of skin a sickly gray-green, I scared even myself.

According to the clock, the Beauty Clay had been on the required twenty minutes, and was now ready to be washed off. It occurred to me that if twenty minutes was enough to make me beautiful, thirty minutes or even forty minutes would make me twice as beautiful. Besides, it would give me more lovely moments of anticipation, and Mother wouldn't be home until after five.

By the time my face was so rigid that even my eyeballs felt yanked from their sockets, I knew I must be done, on both sides. As I started back to the bathroom, I heard Bobby's voice downstairs yelling "Mom!" With the haste born of horror I ran back and just managed to bolt myself inside the bathroom as Bobby leaped up the stairs and came down the hall toward his room. Then I turned on the faucet and set to work. The directions had particularly warned "Use only gentle splashes to remove the mask—No rubbing or washcloth." It took several minutes of gentle splashing to make me realize this was getting me nowhere fast. Indeed, it was like splashing playfully at the Rock of Gibraltar. I decided that maybe it wouldn't hurt if I rubbed the beauty mask just a little, with a nailbrush. This hurt only the nailbrush. I myself remained embedded in Beauty Clay.

By this time, I was getting worried. Mother would be home very soon and I needed a face—even any old face. Suddenly it occurred to me that a silver knife would be a big help, although I wasn't sure just how. When I heard Bobby moving around in his room, I yelled at him to bring me a knife from the dining-room sideboard. Rather, that's what I intended to yell, but my facial muscles were still cast in stone, and the most I could do was grunt. In desperation, I ran down to the sideboard, tripping over my sheet as I went, and got the knife. Unfortunately, just as I was coming back through the dusky upstairs hall, Bobby walked out of his room and met me, face to face. The mental impact, on Bobby, was terrific. To do him justice, he realized almost instantly that this was his own sister, and not, as he at first imagined, a sea monster. But even this realization was not too reassuring.

I had often imagined how my family would look at me after the Beauty Clay had taken effect. Now it had taken effect—or even permanent possession of me—and Bobby was certainly reacting, but not quite as I'd pictured it.

"Wh—what?" he finally managed to croak, pointing at my face.

His concern was so obvious and even comforting that I tried to explain what had happened. The sounds that came out alarmed him even more.

Not having the time or the necessary freedom of speech to explain any further, I dashed into the bathroom and began hitting the handle of the knife against my rocky visage. To my heavenly relief, it began to crack. After repeated blows, which made me a little groggy, the stuff had broken up enough to allow me to wriggle my jaw. Meanwhile, Bobby stood at the door watching, completely bemused.

Taking advantage of the cracks in my surface, I dug the blade of the knife in, and by scraping, gouging, digging and prying, I got part of my face clear. As soon as I could talk, I turned on Bobby. "If you tell anybody about this, I'll kill you," I said fiercely.

Whether it was the intensity of my threat or a latent chivalry aroused by seeing a lady tortured before his very eyes, I still don't know, but Bobby said, "Cross my heart and hope to die."

He then pointed out that spots of the gray-green stuff were still very much with me. As I grabbed up the nailbrush again, to tackle these remnants, he asked in a hushed voice, "But what *is* it?"

"Beauty Clay," I said. "I sent away for it."

Bobby looked as though he couldn't understand why anyone would deliberately send away for such punishment, when there was already enough trouble in the world. However, for the first time in a long, hideous half-hour, I remembered why I'd gone through this ordeal, and now I looked into the mirror expecting to see results that would wipe out all memory of suffering. The reflection that met my eye was certainly changed all right, varying as it did between an angry scarlet where the skin had been rubbed off, to the greenish splotches still clinging.

Maybe if I got it all off, I thought. When it was all off, except those portions wedded to my hair, I gazed at myself wearily, all hope abandoned. My face was my own—but raw. Instead of the Body Beautiful I looked like the Body Boiled. Even worse, my illusions had been cracked wide open, and not by a silver knife.

"You look awfully red," Bobby said. I did indeed. To add to my troubles, we could now hear the family assembling downstairs, and Mother's voice came up, "Hildegarde, will you come set the table right away, dear?"

I moved numbly.

"You'd better take off the sheet," Bobby said.

I took off the sheet.

Just as I reached the stairs, he whispered, "Why don't you say you were frostbitten and rubbed yourself with snow?"

I looked at him with limp gratitude.

When Mother saw my scarlet, splotched face, she exclaimed in concern. "Why, Hildegarde, are you feverish?" She made a move as if to feel my forehead, but I backed away. I was burning up, but not with fever.

"I'm all right," I said, applying myself to setting the table. With my face half in the china cupboard, I mumbled that I'd been frostbitten and had rubbed myself with snow.

"Oh, Cliff," Mother called. "Little Hildegarde was frostbitten."

My father immediately came out to the kitchen. "How could she be frostbitten?" he asked reasonably. "It's thirty-four above zero."

"But her ears still look white," Mother said.

They probably did, too, compared to the rest of my face. By some oversight, I had neglected to put Beauty Clay on my ears. "I'm all right," I insisted again. "I rubbed hard to get the circulation going."

This at least was true. Anyone could tell at a glance that my circulation was going full blast, from the neck up.

Bobby had followed me out to the kitchen to see how the frostbite story went over. As mother kept exclaiming over my condition he now said staunchly, "Sure she's all right. Let her alone."

My father and mother both stared at him, in this new role of Big Brother Galahad. In fact, my father reacted rather cynically. "Bobby, did you and your friends knock Hildegarde down and rub her face with snow?" he asked.

"Me?" Bobby squeaked. He gave me a dirty look, as if to say, "You'd better talk fast."

I denied hotly that Bobby had done any such thing. In fact, I proceeded to build him up as my sole rescuer, a great big St. Bernard of a brother who had come bounding through the snowdrifts to bring me life and hope.

Bobby looked so gratified at what he'd been through in my story that I knew my secret was safe.

Sally, always an affectionate child, began to sob. "She might have died. Bobby saved her from freezing."

My father and mother remained dry-eyed. Against this new set-up of Brother Loves Sister they were suspicious, but inclined to do nothing.

And in a way I *had* been frostbitten, to the quick. Lying in bed that night, still smarting, I tried to think up ways to get even. It wasn't clear to me exactly whom or what I had to get even with. All I knew was that I was sore and unbeautiful, and mulcted of five dollars. With the hot and cold fury of a woman stung, I suddenly conceived my plan for revenge. It was so simple and logical and yet brilliant that my mind relaxed at last. Someday I, too, would write advertisements.

# The Affair at 7, Rue de M——

*by John Steinbeck*

I had hoped to withhold from public scrutiny those rather curious events which have given me some concern for the past month. I knew of course that there was talk in the neighborhood. I have even heard some of the distortions current in my district, stories, I hasten to add, in which there is no particle of truth. However, my desire for privacy was shattered yesterday by a visit of two members of the fourth estate who assured me that the story, or rather a story, had escaped the boundaries of my *arrondisement.*

In the light of impending publicity I think it only fair to issue the true details of those happenings which have come to be known as The Affair at 7, rue de M——, in order that nonsense may not be added to a set of circumstances which are not without their *bizarrerie.* I shall set down the events as they happened without comment, thereby allowing the public to judge of the situation.

At the beginning of the summer I carried my family to Paris and took up residence in a pretty little house at 7, rue de M——, a building which in another period had been the mews of the great house beside it. The whole property is now owned and part of it inhabited by a noble French family of such age and purity that its members still consider the Bourbons unacceptable as claimants to the throne of France.

---

From *Harper's Bazaar.*

To this pretty little converted stable with three floors of rooms above a well-paved courtyard, I brought my immediate family, consisting of my wife, my three children, two small boys and a grown daughter, and of course myself. Our domestic arrangement, in addition to the concierge who, as you might say, came with the house, consists of a French cook of great ability, a Spanish maid and my own secretary, a girl of Swiss nationality whose high attainments and ambitions are only equaled by her moral altitude. This then was our little family group when the events I am about to chronicle were ushered in.

If one must have an agency in this matter, I can find no alternative to placing not the blame but rather the authorship, albeit innocent, on my younger son John, a lively child of singular beauty and buck teeth.

This young man has, during the last several years in America, become not so much an addict as an aficionado of that curious American practice, the chewing of bubble gum, and one of the pleasanter aspects of the early summer in Paris lay in the fact that the Cadet John had neglected to bring any of the atrocious substance with him from America. The child's speech became clear and unobstructed and the hypnotized look went out of his eyes. Alas, this delightful situation was not long to continue. An old family friend traveling in Europe brought as a present to the children a more than adequate supply of this beastly gum, thinking to do them a kindness. Thereupon the old familiar situation reasserted itself. Speech fought its damp way past a huge wad of the gum and emerged with the sound of a faulty water trap. The jaws were in constant motion, giving the face at best a look of agony while the eyes took on a glaze like those of a pig with a recently severed jugular. Since I do not believe in inhibiting my children I resigned myself to a summer not quite so pleasant as I had at first hoped.

On occasion I do not follow my ordinary practice of laissez-faire.

When I am composing the material for a book or play or essay, in a word, when the utmost of concentration is required, I am prone to establish tyrannical rules for my own comfort and effectiveness. One of these rules is that there shall be neither chewing nor bubbling while I am trying to concentrate. This rule is so thoroughly understood by the Cadet John that he accepts it as one of the laws of nature and does not either complain or attempt to evade the ruling. It is his pleasure and my solace for my son to come sometimes into my workroom, there to sit quietly beside me for a time. He knows he must be silent and when he has remained so for as long a time as his character permits, he goes out quietly, leaving us both enriched by the wordless association.

Two weeks ago in the late afternoon, I sat at my desk composing a short essay for *Figaro Littéraire,* an essay which later aroused some controversy when it was printed under the title "Sartre Resartus." I had come to that passage concerning the proper clothing for the soul when to my astonishment and chagrin I heard the unmistakable soft plopping sound of a bursting balloon of bubble gum. I looked sternly at my offspring and saw him chewing away. His cheeks were colored with embarrassment and the muscles of his jaw stood rigidly out.

"You know the rule," I said coldly.

To my amazement tears came into his eyes and while his jaws continued to masticate hugely, his blubbery voice forced its way past the huge lump of bubble gum in his mouth.

"I didn't do it," he cried.

"What do you mean, you didn't do it?" I demanded in a rage. "I distinctly heard and now I distinctly see."

"Oh, sir!" he moaned. "I really didn't. I'm not chewing it, sir. It's chewing me."

For a moment I inspected him closely. He is an honest child, only under the greatest pressure of gain permitting himself an untruth. I had the horrible thought that the bubble gum had finally had its way and that my son's reason was tottering. If this were so, it were better to tread softly. Quietly I put out my hand. "Lay it here," I said kindly.

My child tried manfully to disengage the gum from his jaws. "It won't let me go," he sputtered.

"Open up," I said and then inserting my fingers in his mouth I seized hold of the large lump of gum and after a struggle in which my fingers slipped again and again, managed to drag it forth and to deposit the ugly blob on my desk on top of a pile of white manuscript paper.

For a moment it seemed to shudder there on the paper and then with an easy slowness it began to undulate, to swell and recede with the exact motion of being chewed while my son and I regarded it with popping eyes.

For a long time we watched it while I drove through my mind for some kind of explanation. Either I was dreaming or some principle as yet unknown had taken its seat in the pulsing bubble gum on the desk. I am not unintelligent. While I considered the indecent thing, a hundred little thoughts and glimmerings of understanding raced through my brain. At last I asked, "How long has it been chewing you?"

"Since last night," he replied.

"And when did you first notice, this, this propensity on its part?"

He spoke with perfect candor. "I will ask you to believe me, sir," he said. "Last night before I went to sleep I put it under my pillow as is my invariable custom. In the night I was awakened to find that it was in my mouth. I again placed it under my pillow and this morning it was again in my mouth, lying very quietly. When, however, I became thoroughly awakened, I was conscious of a slight motion and shortly afterward the situation dawned on me that I was no longer master of the gum. It had taken its head. I tried to remove it, sir, and could not. You yourself with all of your strength have seen how difficult it was to extract. I came to your workroom to await your first disengagement, wishing to acquaint you with my difficulty. Oh, Daddy, what do you think has happened?"

The cancerous thing held my complete attention.

"I must think," I said. "This is something a little out of the ordinary, and I do not believe it should be passed over without some investigation."

As I spoke a change came over the gum. It ceased to chew itself and seemed to rest for a while, and then with a flowing movement like those monocellular animals of the order *Paramecium,* the gum slid across the desk straight in the direction of my son. For a moment I was stricken with astonishment and for an even longer time I failed to discern its intent. It dropped to his knee, climbed horribly up his shirt front. Only then did I understand. It was trying to get back into his mouth. He looked down on it paralyzed with fright.

"Stop," I cried, for I realized that my third-born was in danger and at such times I am capable of a violence which verges on the murderous. I seized the monster from his chin and striding from my workroom, entered the salon, opened the window, and hurled the thing into the busy traffic on the rue de M——.

I believe it is the duty of a parent to ward off those shocks which may cause dreams or trauma whenever possible. I went back to my study to find young John sitting where I had left him. He was staring into space. There was a troubled line between his brows.

"Son," I said, "you and I have seen something which, while we know it to have happened, we might find difficult to describe with any degree of success to others. I ask you to imagine the scene if we should tell this story to the other members of the family. I greatly fear we should be laughed out of the house."

"Yes, sir," he said passively.

"Therefore I am going to propose to you, my son, that we lock the episode deep in our memories and never mention it to a soul as long as we live." I waited for his assent and when it did not come, glanced up at his face to see it a ravaged field of terror. His eyes were starting out of his head. I turned in the direction of his gaze. Under the door there crept a paper-thin sheet which, once it had entered the room, grew to a gray blob and rested on the rug, pulsing and chewing. After a moment it moved again by pseudopodian progression toward my son.

I fought down panic as I rushed at it. I grabbed it up and flung it on my desk, then seizing an African war club from among the trophies on the wall, a dreadful instrument studded with brass, I beat the gum until I was breathless and it a torn piece of plastic fabric. The moment I rested, it drew itself together and for a few moments chewed very rapidly as though it chuckled at my impotence, and then inexorably it moved toward my son, who by this time was crouched in a corner moaning with terror.

Now a coldness came over me. I picked up the filthy thing and wrapped it in my handkerchief, strode out of the house, walked three blocks to the Seine and flung the handkerchief into the slowly moving current.

I spent a good part of the afternoon soothing my son and trying to reassure him that his fears were over. But such was his nervousness that I had to give him half a barbiturate tablet to get him to sleep that night, while my wife insisted that I call a doctor. I did not at that time dare to tell her why I could not obey her wish.

I was awakened, indeed the whole house was awakened, in the night by a terrified muffled scream from the children's room. I took the stairs two at a time and burst in the room, flicking the light switch as I went. John sat up in bed squalling, while with his fingers he dug at his half-opened mouth, a mouth which horrifyingly went right on chewing. As I looked a bubble emerged between his fingers and burst with a wet plopping sound.

What chance of keeping our secret now! All had to be explained, but with the plopping gum pinned to a breadboard with an ice pick the explanation was easier than it might have been. And I am proud of the help and comfort given me. There is no strength like that of the family. Our French cook solved the problem by refusing to believe it even when she saw it. It was not reasonable, she explained, and she was a reasonable member of a reasonable people. The Spanish maid ordered and paid for an exorcism by the parish priest who, poor man, after two hours of strenuous effort went away muttering that this was more a matter of the stomach than the soul.

For two weeks we were besieged by the monster. We burned it in the fireplace, causing it to splutter in blue flames and melt in a nasty mess among the ashes. Before morning it had crawled through the keyhole of the children's room, leaving a trail of wood ash on the door, and again we were awakened by screams from the Cadet.

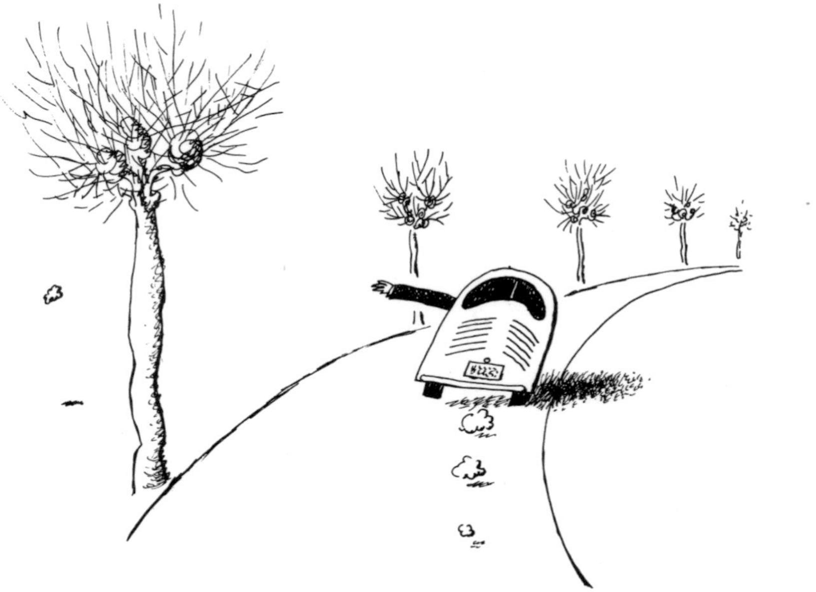

In despair I drove far into the country and threw it from my automobile. It was back before morning. Apparently it had crept to the highway and placed itself in the Paris traffic until picked up by a truck tire. When we tore it from John's mouth it had still the nonskid marks of Michelin imprinted in its side.

Fatigue and frustration will take their toll. In exhaustion, with my will to fight back sapped, and after we had tried every possible method to lose or destroy the bubble gum, I placed it at last under a bell jar which I ordinarily use to cover my microscope. I collapsed in a chair to gaze at it with weary defeated eyes. John slept in his little bed under the influence of sedatives backed by my assurance that I would not let the Thing out of my sight.

I lighted a pipe and settled back to watch it. Inside the bell jar the gray tumorous lump moved restlessly about searching for some means of exit from its prison. Now and then it paused as though in thought and emitted a bubble in my direction. I could feel the hatred it had for me. In my weariness I found my mind slipping into an analysis which had so far escaped me.

The background I had been over hurriedly. It must be that from constant association with the lambent life which is my son, the magic of life had been created in the bubble gum. And with life had come intelligence, not the manly open intelligence of the boy, but an evil calculating wiliness.

How could it be otherwise? Intelligence without the soul to balance it must of necessity be evil. The gum had not absorbed any part of John's soul.

Very well, said my mind, now we have a hypothesis of its origin, let us consider its nature. What does it think? What does it want? What does it need? My mind leaped like a terrier. It needs and wants to get back to its host, my son. It wants to be chewed. It must be chewed to survive.

Inside the bell jar the gum inserted a thin wedge of itself under the heavy glass foot and constricted so that the whole jar lifted a fraction of an inch. I laughed as I drove it back. I laughed with almost insane triumph. I had the answer.

In the dining room I procured a clear plastic plate, one of a dozen my wife had bought for picnics in the country. Then turning the bell jar over and securing the monster in its bottom, I smeared the mouth of it with a heavy plastic cement guaranteed to be water-, alcohol-, and acid-proof. I forced the plate over the opening and pressed it down until the glue took hold and bound the plate to the glass, making an airtight container. And last I turned the jar upright again and adjusted the reading light so that I could observe every movement of my prisoner.

Again it searched the circle for escape. Then it faced me and emitted a great number of bubbles very rapidly. I could hear the little bursting plops through the glass.

"I have you, my beauty," I cried. "I have you at last."

That was a week ago. I have not left the side of the bell jar since, and have only turned my head to accept a cup of coffee. When I go to the bathroom, my wife takes my place. I can now report the following hopeful news.

During the first day and night, the bubble gum tried every means to escape. Then for a day and a night it seemed to be agitated and nervous as though it had for the first time realized its predicament. The third day it went to work with its chewing motion, only the action was speeded up greatly, like the chewing of a baseball fan. On the fourth day it began to weaken and I observed with joy a kind of dryness on its once slick and shiny exterior.

I am now in the seventh day and I believe it is almost over. The gum is lying in the center of the plate. At intervals it heaves and subsides. Its color has turned to a nasty yellow. Once today when my son entered the room, it leaped up excitedly, then seemed to realize its hopelessness and collapsed on the plate. It will die tonight I think and only then will I dig a deep hole in the garden, and I will deposit the sealed bell jar and cover it up and plant geraniums over it.

It is my hope that this account will set straight some of the silly tales that are being hawked in the neighborhood.

# Father Opens My Mail

*by Clarence Day*

There was a time in my boyhood when I felt that Father had handicapped me severely in life by naming me after him, "Clarence." All literature, so far as I could see, was thronged with objectionable persons named Clarence. Percy was bad enough, but there had been some good fighters named Percy. The only Clarence in history was a duke who did something dirty at Tewkesbury, and who died a ridiculous death afterwards in a barrel of malmsey.

As for the Clarences in the fiction I read, they were horrible. In one story, for instance, there were two brothers, Clarence and Frank. Clarence was a "vain, disagreeable little fellow," who was proud of his curly hair and fine clothes, while Frank was a "rollicking boy who was ready to play games with anybody." Clarence didn't like to play games, of course. He just minced around looking on.

One day when the mother of these boys had gone out, this story went on, Clarence "tempted" Frank to disobey her and fly their kite on the roof. Frank didn't want to, but Clarence kept taunting him and daring him until Frank was stung into doing it. After the two boys went up to the roof, Frank got good and dirty, running up and down and stumbling over scuttles, while Clarence sat there, giving him orders, and kept his natty clothes tidy. To my horror, he even spread out his handkerchief on the trapdoor to sit on. And to crown all, this sneak told on Frank as soon as their mother came in.

This wasn't an exceptionally mean Clarence, either. He was just run-of-the-mill. Some were worse.

---

From *Life With Father*.

327-
1792

#141 [illegible] 2

d and save harmless the State, its officers, agents
s accruing or resulting to any and all contractors,
other person, firm or corporation furnishing or
connection with the performance of this contract,
g or resulting to any person, firm or corporation
or in the performance of this contract.

oyees of Contractor, in the performance of this
y and not as officers or employees or agents of

d be relieved of the payment of any consideration
n the covenants herein contained at the time and
such termination the State may proceed with the
te. The cost to the State shall be deducted from
ment, and the balance, if any, shall be paid the

, this agreement is not assignable by Contractor

So far as I could ever learn, however, Father had never heard of these stories, and had never dreamed of there being anything objectionable in his name. Quite the contrary. And yet as a boy he had lived a good rough-and-tumble boy's life. He had played and fought on the city streets, and kept a dog in Grandpa's stable, and stolen rides to Greenpoint Ferry on the high, lurching bus. In the summer he had gone to West Springfield and had run down Shad Lane through the trees to the house where Grandpa was born, and had gone barefoot and driven the cows home just as though he had been named Tom or Bill.

He had the same character as a boy, I suppose, that he had as a man, and he was too independent to care if people thought his name fancy. He paid no attention to the prejudices of others, except to disapprove of them. He had plenty of prejudices himself, of course, but they were his own. He was humorous and confident and level-headed, and I imagine that if any boy had tried to make fun of him for being named Clarence, Father would simply have laughed and told him he didn't know what he was talking about.

I asked Mother how this name had ever happened to spring up in our family. She explained that my great-great-grandfather was Benjamin Day, and my great-grandfather was Henry, and consequently my grandfather had been named Benjamin Henry. He in turn had named his eldest son Henry and his second son Benjamin. The result was that when Father was born there was no family name left. The privilege of choosing a name for Father had thereupon been given to Grandma, and unluckily for the Day family she had been reading a novel, the hero of which was named Clarence.

I knew that Grandma, though very like Grandpa in some respects, had a dreamy side which he hadn't, a side that she usually kept to herself, in her serene, quiet way. Her romantic choice of this name probably made Grandpa smile, but he was a detached sort of man who didn't take small matters seriously, and who drew a good deal of private amusement from the happenings of everyday life. Besides, he was partly to blame in this case, because that novel was one he had published himself in his magazine.

I asked Mother, when she had finished, why I had been named Clarence too.

It hadn't been her choice, Mother said. She had suggested all sorts of names to Father, but there seemed to be something wrong with each one. When she had at last spoken of naming me after him, he had said at once that that was the best suggestion yet—he said it sounded just right.

Father and I would have had plenty of friction in any case. This identity of names made things worse. Every time that I had been more of a fool than he liked, Father would try to impress on me my responsibilities as his eldest son, and above all as the son to whom he had given his name, as he put it. A great deal was expected, it seemed to me, of a boy who was named after his father. I used to envy my brothers, who didn't have anything expected of them on this score at all.

I envied them still more after I was old enough to begin getting letters. I then discovered that when Father "gave" me his name, he had also, not unnaturally, I had to admit, retained it himself, and when anything came for Clarence S. Day he opened it, though it was sometimes for me.

He also opened everything that came addressed to Clarence S. Day, Jr. He didn't do this intentionally, but unless the "Jr." was clearly written, it looked like "Esq.," and anyhow Father was too accustomed to open all Clarence Day letters to remember about looking carefully every time for a "Jr." So far as mail and express went, I had no name at all of my own.

For the most part nobody wrote to me when I was a small boy except firms whose advertisements I had read in the *Youth's Companion* and to whom I had written requesting them to send me their circulars. These circulars described remarkable bargains in magicians' card outfits, stamps and coins, pocket knives, trick spiders, and imitation fried eggs, and they seemed interesting and valuable to me when I got them. The trouble was that Father usually got them and at once tore them up. I then had to write for such circulars again, and if Father got the second one too, he would sometimes explode with annoyance. He became particularly indignant one year, I remember, when he was repeatedly urged to take advantage of a special bargain sale of false whiskers. He said he couldn't understand why these offerings kept pouring in. I knew why, in this case, but at other times I was often surprised myself at the number he got, not realizing that as a result of my postcard request my or our name had been automatically put on several large general mailing lists.

During this period I got more of my mail out of Father's wastebasket than I did from the postman.

At the age of twelve or thirteen, I stopped writing for these childish things and turned to a new field. Father and I, whichever of us got at the mail first, then began to receive not merely circulars but personal letters beginning:

Dear Friend Day:

In reply to your valued request for one of our Mammoth Agents' Outfits, kindly forward postoffice order for $1.49 to cover cost of postage and packing, and we will put you in a position to earn a large income in your spare time with absolutely no labor on your part, by taking subscriptions for *The Secret Handbook of Mesmerism,* and our *Tales of Blood* series.

And one spring, I remember, as the result of what I had intended to be a secret application on my part, Father was assigned "the exclusive rights for Staten Island and Hoboken of selling the Gem Home Popper for Pop Corn. Housewives buy it at sight."

After Father had stormily endured these afflictions for a while, he and I began to get letters from girls. Fortunately for our feelings, these were rare, but they were ordeals for both of us. Father had forgotten, if he ever knew, how silly young girls can sound, and I got my first lesson in how unsystematic they were. No matter how private and playful they meant their letters to be, they forgot to put "Jr." on the envelope every once in so often. When Father opened these letters, he read them all the way through, sometimes twice, muttering to himself over and over: "This is very peculiar. I don't understand this at all. Here's a letter to me from some person I never heard of. I can't see what it's about." By the time it had occurred to him that possibly the letter might be for me, I was red and embarrassed and even angrier at the girl than at Father. And on days when he had read some of the phrases aloud to the family, it nearly killed me to claim it.

Lots of fellows whom I knew had been named after their fathers without having such troubles. But although Father couldn't have been kinder-hearted or had any better intentions, when he saw his name on a package or envelope it never dawned on him that it might not be for him. He was too active in his habits to wait until I had a chance to get at it. And as he was also single-minded and prompt to attend to unfinished business, he opened everything automatically and then did his best to dispose of it.

This went on even after I grew up, until I had a home of my own. Father was always perfectly decent about it, but he never changed. When he saw I felt sulky, he was genuinely sorry and said so, but he couldn't see why all this should annoy me, and he was surprised and amused that it did. I used to get angry once in a while when something came for me which I particularly hadn't wished him to see and which I would find lying, opened, on the hall table marked

"For Jr.? " when I came in; but nobody could stay angry with Father—he was too utterly guiltless of having meant to offend.

He often got angry himself, but it was mostly at things, not at persons, and he didn't mind a bit (as a rule) when persons got angry at him. He even declared, when I got back from college, feeling dignified, and told him that I wished he'd be more careful, that he suffered from these mistakes more than I did. It wasn't *his* fault, he pointed out, if my stupid correspondents couldn't remember my name, and it wasn't any pleasure to him to be upset at his breakfast by finding that a damned lunatic company in Battle Creek had sent him a box of dry bread crumbs, with a letter asserting that this rubbish would be good for his stomach. "I admit I threw it into the fireplace, Clarence, but what else could I do? If you valued this preposterous concoction, my dear boy, I'm sorry. I'll buy another box for you today, if you'll tell me where I can get it. Don't feel badly. I'll buy you a barrel. Only I hope you won't eat it."

In the days when Mrs. Pankhurst and her friends were chaining themselves to lamp-posts in London, in their campaign for the vote, a letter came from Frances Hand trustfully asking "Dear Clarence" to do something to help Woman Suffrage—speak at a meeting, I think. Father got red in the face. "Speak at one of their meetings!" he roared at Mother. "I'd like nothing better! You can tell Mrs. Hand that it would give me great pleasure to inform all those crackpots in petticoats exactly what I think of their antics."

"Now, Clare," Mother said, "you mustn't talk that way. I like that nice Mrs. Hand, and anyhow this letter must be for Clarence."

One time I asked Father for his opinion of a low-priced stock I'd been watching. His opinion was that it was not worth a damn. I thought this over, but I still wished to buy it, so I placed a scale order with another firm instead of with Father's office, and said nothing about it. At the end of the month this other firm sent me a statement, setting forth each of my little transactions in full, and of course they forgot to put the "Jr." at the end of my name. When Father opened the envelope, he thought at first in his excitement that this firm had actually opened an account for him without being asked. I found him telling Mother that he'd like to wring their damned necks.

"That must be for me, Father," I said, when I took in what had happened.

We looked at each other.

"You bought this stuff?" he said incredulously. "After all I said about it?"

"Yes, Father."

He handed over the statement and walked out of the room.

Both he and I felt offended and angry. We stayed so for several days, too, but we then made it up.

Once in a while when I got a letter that I had no time to answer I used to address an envelope to the sender and then put anything in it that happened to be lying around on my desk—a circular about books, a piece of newspaper, an old laundry bill—anything at all, just to be amiable, and yet at the same time to save myself the trouble of writing. I happened to tell several people about this private habit of mine at a dinner one night—a dinner at which Alice Duer Miller and one or two other writers were present. A little later she wrote me a criticism of Henry James and ended by saying that I needn't send her any of my old laundry bills because she wouldn't stand it. And she forgot to put on the "Jr."

"In the name of God," Father said bleakly, "this is the worst yet. Here's a woman who says I'd better not read *The Golden Bowl,* which I have no intention whatever of doing, and she also warns me for some unknown reason not to send her my laundry bills."

The good part of all these experiences, as I realize now, was that in the end they drew Father and me closer together. My brothers had only chance battles with him. I had a war. Neither he nor I relished its clashes, but they made us surprisingly intimate.

# Child's Play

*A Selection of Anecdotes as Told by Bennett Cerf*

A young mother in Milwaukee, exhausted from her daily chores, lay down on her couch to steal forty winks. Half asleep, she felt one of her youngsters patting her face and was drowsily pleased by this unexpected display of affection.

Then the doorbell rang. She jumped up with a start to admit a delivery man from her husband's favorite tobacco shop. He looked at her so queerly that when he had gone, she rushed over to a mirror to inspect herself.

Her face was completely plastered with green trading stamps!

There's a lady in the suburbs who is determined that, when her twelve-year-old son Herbert grows up, he will be not only a superb dancer, but a brilliant conversationalist as well. With that end in view, she marches him to dancing school every Wednesday afternoon, and furthermore sits grimly at the ringside to see that he not only pushes little girls around the room, more or less in tune with the music, but talks to them brightly at the same time. Herbert takes an exceedingly dim view of the entire procedure.

Last Wednesday, Herbert was executing what he fondly believed to be a foxtrot with a brand-new dancing partner when he caught his mother's signal: "Engage her in conversation!" He took a deep breath, and gallantly informed his lady fair, "Say, you sweat less than any fat girl I've ever danced with!"

A fond mother was pleased with her son. "You see, Jerry," she

---

From *Try and Stop Me* and other books by Bennett Cerf.

beamed, "I told you that was a nice little boy next door. I was glad to see from the window just now that you had made friends with him and were helping him pick up his marbles."

"Marbles!" scoffed Jerry. "I socked him in the jaw. Those weren't marbles; those were teeth."

A girl in the booth at a big movie theatre hesitated when a youngster sought to buy a ticket for the early afternoon show. "Why aren't you in school?" she asked sharply. "It's okay, lady," he assured her. "I've got the measles."

CHILDREN OF DISTINCTION

BOYS

1. Peter, who, like all six-year-olds, abhorred washing, came to the dinner table one evening with elbows black as pitch. Sent back to the bathroom for repairs, he dawdled there so long that his mother called, "How are you coming, Pete? Elbows clean yet?" "Not clean," he called back triumphantly, "but I've got them to match."

2. The 150-pound ten-year-old who won the part of Cleopatra in a school play. "But why," asked his mother, "did they give such a part to the huskiest lad in the class?" "They had to," explained the boy cheerfully. "It was my snake!"

3. The boy scout who admitted to his father that his daily good deed was not quite good enough this once. "I helped an old lady across the street like you suggested," he said, "but she got hit by a taxi."

4. The nine-year-old who, asked by his teacher to name the four seasons of the year, came up with "Football, Basketball, Baseball, and Vacation."

5. The kid from Texas who got all the way to the finals of a national spelling bee but then lost out because he couldn't spell "small."

GIRLS

1. Lucinda, who, at the age of ten was given a check for twenty dollars by her parents and told to open an account at the savings bank. Officials there gave her an application blank that included the question, "Have you had an account previously elsewhere, and if so, will you please print here the name of the bank?"

Lucinda gave the problem due thought, then laboriously spelled out, "Yes. Piggy."

2. The little girl at camp who asked her tentmate, "Do you ever get homesick?" "Yes, I do," admitted the tentmate, "but only when I'm home."

3. The honest seven-year-old who admitted calmly to her parents that Billy Brown had kissed her after class. "How did that happen?" gasped her mother. "It wasn't easy," admitted the young lady, "but three girls helped me catch him."

4. The little girl who assured her teacher, "Of *course* I know how to spell banana. I just never know when to stop."

5. Judy, who was leading her young friends in the kitchen in a symphony banged out on pots and pans. "I wish Mom would hurry

and make us stop," she grumbled. "This noise is killing me."

AND THEIR PARENTS

1. The mother who demanded of her son, just turned seven, "What are you reading?" "A story about a cow jumping over the moon," was the answer. "Throw that book away at once," commanded the mother. "How often have I told you you're too young to read science fiction?"

2. The proud mother who bragged, "My son Arthur is smarter than Abraham Lincoln. Arthur could recite the Gettysburg Address when he was ten years old. Lincoln didn't say it till he was fifty."

3. The dapper New Yorker—one of the ten best-dressed men in America—who came to collect his six-year-old daughter at a birthday party. Taking hold of her hand to guide her across the street, he observed, "Goodness, Vicki, your hands seem mighty sticky today." "Yours would be, too," she informed him, "if you had a piece of lemon pie and a chocolate eclair in your pocket."

4. Will Rogers' ma. When he was ten, she had trouble persuading him to tuck in his shirttails in school or when company came to dinner. Then she sewed lace around the bottom of every shirt he owned. It worked wonders.

5. The mother of little John Charles, who found his first report card distinctly encouraging. "John Charles is a bright, alert lad," was the teacher's comment, "but I believe he spends too much time playing with the girls. However, I am working on a plan which I believe will break him of the habit."

John Charles' mother acknowledged receipt of the report and added this note of her own: "Let me know if your plan works, and I'll try it on his father."

Five-year-old Christopher went to a party in a brand-new suit. When he came home, ragged holes had been cut into it with a pair of scissors. His shocked mother exclaimed, "What did you do to your expensive new suit?"

"We decided to play grocery store," explained Christopher. "I was a piece of Swiss cheese."

A famous film producer's son came home from his freshman year at college with a set of grades so dazzling that the whole family glowed with pride. His brother Jonathan, aged five, finally felt it was time for him to get into the act, however, and declared loudly, "I got an 'A' in arithmetic today."

His father indulgently replied, "I didn't know they taught arithmetic in kindergarten. What's one and one?" Jonathan pondered a moment, then reported, "We haven't gotten that far yet."

A young blueblood from Boston was showing her family album to some friends from the Midwest. "Isn't this one a scream?" she asked. "It's my Aunt Dorothy. She's the fattest lady who ever lived on Pinckney Street." One of the visitors, duly impressed, said, "And who is that standing behind her?" The little girl said, "Don't be silly. That's still Aunt Dorothy."

A little boy had been pawing over a stationer's stock of greeting cards for some time when a clerk asked, "Just what is it you're looking for, Sonny? Birthday greeting? Message to a sick friend? Anniversary congratulations to your ma and dad?"

The boy shook his head "No" and answered wistfully, "Got anything in the line of blank report cards?"

A bank robber was reported driving like mad somewhere in Virginia, and every sheriff in the state was alerted to watch for him. Taking no chances, one conscientious sheriff decided to stop every car on the road and cross-examine its occupants. The dowager in a sleek limousine took this amiss. "By what authority do you presume to stop this car?" she demanded angrily.

The sheriff took his badge out of his pocket to show the lady—and blushed violently. The badge was a tin affair marked "Space

Ship Patrol." His nine-year-old son had switched badges.

Kids dearly love receiving presents—but hate even more having to write thank-you letters therefor. My own Jonny got around to thanking his Uncle Herbert for a Christmas gift along about March 25. What he wrote was, "I'm sorry I didn't thank you for my present, and it would serve me right if you forgot about my birthday next Thursday. . . ."

Here are a couple of noteworthy letters received by fond parents from their children in summer camp:

1. "Dear Mom: Please bring some food when you come to visit me. All we get here is breakfast, lunch, and supper."
2. "Dear Dad: Please write often even if it is only a couple of dollars."

It was Mrs. Abernathy's eleven-year-old daughter, Nell, incidentally, who came home from camp with a gold medal for packing her trunk more neatly than any other girl. "How did you do it?" marveled Mrs. Abernathy, "when at home we can never get you to clean up the mess you leave behind."

"It was cinchy," explained Nell. "I just never unpacked all summer."

A San Francisco six-year-old, obviously impeccably reared, came home from a party in fine spirits, to be asked by his mother, "Were you the youngest one there?"

"Not at all," he answered loftily. "There was another gentleman present who was wheeled in in a baby carriage."

Eight-year-old Claudia was packed off to Charlevoix for a visit with her old-maid aunt. Her last-minute instructions were, "Remember, Aunt Hester is a bit on the prissy side. If you have to go to the bathroom, be sure to say, 'I'd like to powder my nose.'"

Claudia made such a hit with Aunt Hester that when the time came for her to leave she was told, "I certainly loved having you here, my dear. On your next visit you must bring your little sister Sue with you." "I better not," said Claudia hastily. "Sue still powders her nose in bed."

Boys and girls have adopted enthusiastically a game introduced by Steve Allen. Steve provides you with the answer; you must figure out the question.

Examples:

1. *Answer:* Mount Whitney, Mount Olympus, and Mount Sinai.
   *Question:* Name two mountains and a hospital.
2. *Answer:* Cleopatra, Pocahontas, and Florence Nightingale.
   *Question:* Name three dead women.
3. *Answer:* Washington Irving.
   *Question:* Who was the first President, Sam?

Television has changed schoolboys and girls a lot—but they've never come up with a substitute for that good old kissing game of post office. A group of enthusiastic kids were playing it recently at a party, when a boy and girl shut themselves in a closet and didn't come out. "Come out of there," ordered the host's mother finally. "We can't," the boy called back. "We have our braces hooked!"

Nine-year-old Marian, taken by her parents for her first transcontinental rail journey, was thrilled when the train plunged into a long tunnel in the Rockies. When it finally emerged at the other end, she peered out of the vista-dome window, and exclaimed, "Look, Mom! It's tomorrow!"

Herman Hickman, late football coach and commentator, had a sentimental streak almost as wide as he was. Here's his favorite poem, authorship unknown, which he was ready to recite at the drop of a referee's whistle:

A LITTLE BOY PRAYS FOR HIS DOG

Dear God,
They say my dog is dead;
He had the softest little head;
He was so good, he'd always do
Most anything I told him to.

Kind God,
Sometimes he'd chase a cat,
(He wasn't often bad like that),
And if I called him back, he came
The minute that I said his name.

Please God,
If he feels scared up there,
Won't You please let him sleep somewhere
Near You? Oh, please take care of him,
I love him so! His name is Tim.

An amiable gentleman paused to watch some kids in a sandlot baseball game. "What's the score, son?" he asked one of the players. "28 to 0 against us right now," said the kid. "My!" said the gentleman, "Aren't you a bit discouraged?" "Discouraged nothing," enthused the kid. "We haven't been to bat yet."

Never in real life was there a baseball star to compare with one invented by Ed Gardner. His name was Gruskin and he was called Two-Top for the very good reason that he had two heads. This not only enabled him to watch first base and third base at the same time, but made him a great man to pitch double-headers.

When Two-Top Gruskin first reported to the Dodgers he was wearing a white sweater. "What are you fellows staring at?" he asked his new teammates angrily. "Haven't any of you seen a white sweater before?" "Two-Top," interrupted the manager, "I'm a

Thunderherd Day," said Curtis. "With a name like that, you'll get people from all over the country pouring in to see the fireworks."

But no fireworks were contemplated, Standish explained.

"I know, Myles," said Curtis. "I wanted to talk to you about that. You say you want to have a little worship, then have the Indians in for turkey and pumpkin pie. It's a great idea. But, believe me, Myles, it's strictly a nothing bit."

Standish asked what was wrong with it.

"Turkey, Myles. Turkey! You know who eats turkey? Frenchmen. But they call it pheasant, or guinea hen. You're living in *red meat* country, Miles. How are you going to put this colony on the map by sitting around eating turkey? We'll ship in a load of buffalo steak from out West. Then you'll be able to throw a Thunderherd Day with point to it."

Standish asked whether it would hurt the image to invite the Indians.

"Indians!" snorted Curtis. "You're still in the 16th century, Myles. Wait a minute." He entered a convenient dressing room and reappeared a few minutes later wearing a red jacket, red knickers, red nightcap, white beard and black boots.

*"Santa Claus,* Myles! On Thunderherd Day, Santa Claus is going to arrive—right here in Plymouth Colony, with eight tiny reindeer."

Myles said he could not understand how Santa Claus related to the festivities of Thunderherd Day.

"This colony," said Curtis, "is going to be packed with tourists who have come in to be part of Thunderherd Day, part of red-meat country. Their pockets are going to be loaded with wampum. What do we do? Deliver old Santa Claus, to sell them beads and souvenir Pilgrim blunderbusses and those funny black hats you fellows wear. They're going to need Christmas presents anyhow, and the more you can get them to buy right here, the sooner Plymouth Colony is going to move up to dynamic living."

Standish pointed out that Thunderherd Day would occur a full month before Christmas, and it was unlikely that anyone would spend good wampum so long before the holiday.

"You're exactly right, Myles," said Curtis. "And that is why Thunderherd Day is not going to be just one single isolated day on the calendar. *It is going to be the kickoff day for Thunderherd Month."*

That night Myles, John Alden and the others thought it over. "There be no doubt," said a church elder, "that this Curtis knoweth whereof he speaketh, but the question be whether we on this rocky shore truly wish to be held responsible for creating Thunderherd Month."

"Speaking for myself," said John Alden, "I think the image would be very bad."

And so, three centuries elapsed before Thunderherd Month was finally created.

How the first Thanksgiving was salvaged, image-wise

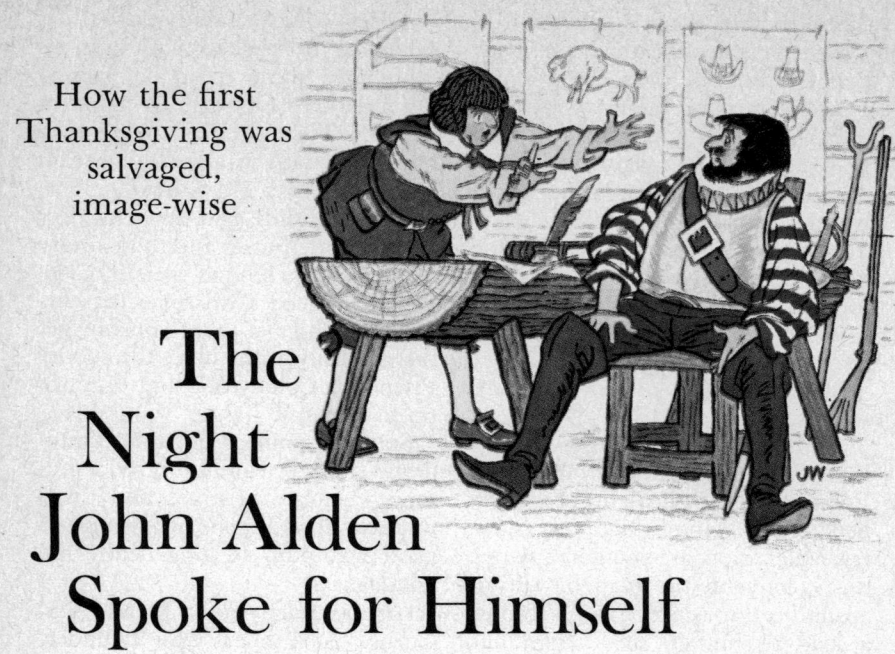

# The Night John Alden Spoke for Himself

*Condensed from* New York Times

Russell Baker

When Custis Curtis, public-relations man for the Plymouth Colony, heard that Myles Standish and his colleagues were planning a day of Thanksgiving, he hopped the first horse to Plymouth Rock.

"Myles," he said, "it's a sweet idea and I love it. There's just one thing: it's all wrong for this particular colony. In the first place, you've got to come up with a better name."

"What's wrong with calling it Thanksgiving?" asked Standish.

"It has no dynamism, Myles, no thunder. This is a big country for big men capable of big dreams. When people think of Plymouth Colony, you want them to think of he-men roaring through Marlboro country with tigers in their cougar tanks. But what does 'Thanksgiving' suggest? Pussycats."

If the name created a too passive image, Standish said, the colony was open to suggestions. "We'll call it

NEW YORK TIMES (NOVEMBER 23, '66), © 1966 BY THE NEW YORK TIMES CO., TIMES SQUARE, NEW YORK, N.Y. 10036 man of few words. There's a uniform and two caps waiting for you. Waiter, bring my new pitcher two glasses of milk."

Two-Top had pitched six hitless innings in his first game when the umpire suddenly threw off his mask and yelled to the manager, "Hey, do you realize this pitcher of yours has two heads?" "Yeah," chimed in the catcher, Gorilla Hogan, "and I'm sick and tired of him already. When I signal for a high fast one, he nods 'yes' with one head, but shakes the other 'no.' Either he goes or I go, Mr. Manager—and don't forget who owns the ball."

That marked the end of Two-Top Gruskin's big-league career, but that very night he won first prize at a masquerade party by disguising himself as a pair of bookends. Then he enlisted in the army. The doctor took his chart to the colonel. "Let's see," said the colonel. "Eyes—brown and blue. Hair—blonde and brunette. Mustache—yes and no. This fellow sounds as if he's got two heads." "He has," said the doctor. "Oh," said the colonel.

Two-Top was a big success in the army as soon as he made up his mind which head to salute.

# How We Kept Mother's Day

*by Stephen Leacock*

Of all the different ideas that have been started lately, I think that the very best is the notion of celebrating once a year "Mother's Day." I don't wonder that this is becoming such a popular day all over America and I am sure the idea will spread to England too.

It is especially in a big family like ours that such an idea takes hold. So we decided to have a special celebration of Mother's Day. We thought it a fine idea. It made us all realize how much Mother had done for us for years, and all the efforts and sacrifice that she had made for our sake.

So we decided that we'd make it a great day, a holiday for all the family, and do everything we could to make Mother happy. Father decided to take a holiday from his office so as to help in celebrating the day, and my sister Anne and I stayed home from college classes, and Mary and my brother Will stayed home from High School.

It was our plan to make it a day just like Xmas or any big holiday, and so we decided to decorate the house with flowers and with mottoes over the mantelpieces, and all that kind of thing. We got Mother to make mottoes and arrange the decorations, because she always does it at Xmas.

The two girls thought it would be a nice thing to dress in our very best for such a big occasion, and so they both got new hats. Mother trimmed both the hats, and they looked fine, and Father

---

From *Laugh With Leacock*.

had bought four-in-hand silk ties for himself and us boys as a souvenir of the day to remember Mother by. We were going to get Mother a new hat too, but it turned out that she seemed to really like her old grey bonnet better than a new one, and both the girls said that it was awfully becoming to her.

Well, after breakfast we had it arranged as a surprise for Mother that we would hire a motor car and take her for a beautiful drive away into the country. Mother is hardly ever able to have a treat like that, because we can only afford to keep one maid, and so Mother is busy in the house nearly all the time. And of course the country is so lovely now that it would be just grand for her to have a lovely morning, driving for miles and miles.

But on the very morning of the day we changed the plan a little bit, because it occurred to Father that a thing it would be better to do even than to take Mother for a motor drive would be to take her fishing. Father said that as the car was hired and paid for, we might just as well use it for a drive up into hills where the streams are. As Father said, if you just go out driving without any object, you have a sense of aimlessness, but if you are going to fish, there is a definite purpose in front of you to heighten the enjoyment.

So we all felt that it would be nicer for Mother to have a definite purpose; and anyway, it turned out that Father had just got a new rod the day before, which made the idea of fishing all the more appropriate, and he said that Mother could use it if she wanted to; in fact, he said it was practically for her, only Mother said she would much rather watch him fish and not try to fish herself.

So we got everything arranged for the trip, and we got Mother to cut up some sandwiches and make up a sort of lunch in case we got hungry, though of course we were to come back home to a big dinner in the middle of the day, just like Xmas or New Year's Day. Mother packed it all up in a basket for us ready to go in the motor.

Well, when the car came to the door, it turned out that there hardly seemed as much room in it as we had supposed, because we hadn't reckoned on Father's fishing basket and the rods and the lunch, and it was plain enough that we couldn't all get in.

Father said not to mind him, he said that he could just as well stay home, and that he was sure that he could put in the time working in the garden; he said that there was a lot of rough dirty work that he could do, like digging a trench for the garbage, that would save hiring a man, and so he said that he'd stay home; he said that we were not to let the fact of his not having had a real holiday for three years stand in our way; he wanted us to go right ahead and be happy and have a big day, and not to mind him. He said that he could plug away all day, and in fact he said he'd been a fool to think there'd be any holiday for him.

But of course we all felt that it would never do to let Father stay home, especially as we knew he would make trouble if he did. The two girls, Anne and Mary, would gladly have stayed and helped the maid get dinner, only it seemed such a pity to, on a lovely day like this, having their new hats. But they both said that Mother had only to say the word, and they'd gladly stay home and work. Will and I would have dropped out, but unfortunately we wouldn't have been any use in getting the dinner.

So in the end it was decided that Mother would stay home and just have a lovely restful day round the house, and get the dinner. It turned out anyway that Mother doesn't care for fishing, and also it was just a little bit cold and fresh out of doors, though it was lovely and sunny, and Father was rather afraid that Mother might take cold if she came.

He said he would never forgive himself if he dragged Mother round the country and let her take a severe cold at a time when she might be having a beautiful rest. He said it was our duty to try and let Mother get all the rest and quiet that she could, after all that she had done for all of us, and he said that that was principally why he had fallen in with this idea of a fishing trip, so as to give Mother a little quiet. He said that young people seldom realize how much quiet means to people who are getting old. As to himself, he could still stand the racket, but he was glad to shelter Mother from it.

So we all drove away with three cheers for Mother, and Mother stood and watched us from the verandah for as long as she could see us, and Father waved his hand back to her every few minutes till he hit his hand on the back edge of the car, and then said that he didn't think that Mother could see us any longer.

Well, we had the loveliest day up among the hills that you could possibly imagine, and Father caught such big specimens that he felt sure that Mother couldn't have landed them anyway, if she had been fishing for them, and Will and I fished too, though we didn't get so many as Father, and the two girls met quite a lot of people that they knew as we drove along, and there were some young men friends of theirs that they met along the stream and talked to, and so we all had a splendid time.

It was quite late when we got back, nearly seven o'clock in the evening, but Mother had guessed that we would be late, so she had kept back the dinner so as to have it just nicely ready and hot for us. Only first she had to get towels and soap for Father and clean things for him to put on, because he always gets so messed up with fishing, and that kept Mother busy for a little while, that and helping the girls get ready.

But at last everything was ready, and we sat down to the grandest kind of dinner—roast turkey and all sorts of things like on Xmas Day. Mother had to get up and down a good bit during the meal fetching things back and forward, but at the end Father noticed it and said she simply mustn't do it, that he wanted her to spare herself, and he got up and fetched the walnuts over from the sideboard himself.

The dinner lasted a long while, and was great fun, and when it was over all of us wanted to help clear the things up and wash the dishes, only Mother said that she would really much rather do it, and so we let her, because we wanted just for once to humor her.

It was quite late when it was all over, and when we all kissed Mother before going to bed, she said it had been the most wonderful day in her life, and I think there were tears in her eyes. So we all felt awfully repaid for all that we had done.

# Your Boy and His Dog

*by Robert Benchley*

People are constantly writing in to this department and asking: "What kind of dog shall I give my boy?" or sometimes: "What kind of boy shall I give my dog?" And although we are always somewhat surprised to get a query like this, ours really being the Jam and Fern Question Box, we usually give the same answer to both forms of inquiry: "Are you quite sure that you want to do either?" This confuses them, and we are able to snatch a few more minutes for our regular work.

But the question of Boy and Dog is one which will not be downed. There is no doubt that every healthy, normal boy (if there is such a thing in these days of Child Study) should own a dog at some time in his life, preferably between the ages of forty-five and fifty. Give a dog to a boy who is much younger and his parents will find themselves obliged to pack up and go to the Sailors' Snug Harbor to live until the dog runs away—which he will do as soon as the first pretty face comes along.

But a dog teaches a boy fidelity, perseverance, and to turn around three times before lying down—very important traits in times like these. In fact, just as soon as a dog comes along who, in addition to these qualities, also knows when to buy and sell stocks, he can be moved right up to the boy's bedroom and the boy can sleep in the doghouse.

In buying a dog for a very small child, attention must be paid to one or two essential points. In the first place, the dog must be one which will come apart easily or of such a breed that the sizing will

---

From *Chips Off the Old Benchley.*

get pasty and all gummed up when wet. Dachshunds are ideal dogs for small children, as they are already stretched and pulled to such a length that the child cannot do much harm one way or the other. The dachshund being so long also makes it difficult for a very small child to go through with the favorite juvenile maneuver of lifting the dog's hind legs up in the air and wheeling it along like a barrow, cooing, "Diddy-app!" Any small child trying to lift a dachshund's hind legs up very high is going to find itself flat on its back.

For the very small child who likes to pick animals up around the middle and carry them over to the fireplace, mastiffs, St. Bernards, or Russian wolfhounds are not indicated—that is, not if the child is of any value at all. It is not that the larger dogs resent being carried around the middle and dropped in the fireplace (in fact, the smaller the dog, the more touchy it is in matters of dignity, as is so often the case with people and nations); but, even though a mastiff does everything that it can to help the child in carrying it by the diaphragm, there are matters of gravity to be reckoned with which make it impossible to carry the thing through without something being broken. If a dog could be trained to wrestle and throw the child immediately, a great deal of time could be saved.

But, as we have suggested, the ideal age for a boy to own a dog is between forty-five and fifty. By this time the boy ought to have attained his full growth and, provided he is ever going to, ought to know more or less what he wants to make of himself in life. At this age the dog will be more of a companion than a chattel, and, if necessary, can be counted upon to carry the boy by the middle and drop him into bed in case sleep overcomes him at a dinner or camp meeting or anything. It can also be counted upon to tell him he has made a fool of himself and embarrassed all his friends. A wife could do no more.

The training of the dog is something which should be left to the boy, as this teaches him responsibility and accustoms him to the use of authority, probably the only time he will ever have a chance to use it. If, for example, the dog insists on following the boy when he is leaving the house, even after repeated commands to "Go on back home!" the boy must decide on one of two courses. He must either take the dog back to the house and lock it in the cellar, or, as an alternate course, he can give up the idea of going out himself and stay with the dog. The latter is the better way, especially if the dog is in good voice and given to screaming the house down.

There has always been considerable difference of opinion as to whether or not a dog really thinks. I, personally, have no doubt that distinct mental processes do go on inside the dog's brain, although many times these processes are hardly worthy of the name. I have known dogs, especially puppies, who were almost as stupid as humans in their mental reactions.

The only reason that puppies do not get into more trouble than they do (if there *is* any more trouble than that which puppies get into) is that they are so small. A child, for instance, should not expect to be able to fall as heavily, eat as heartily of shoe leather, or throw up as casually as a puppy does, for there is more bulk to a child and the results of these practices will be more serious in exact proportion to the size and capacity. Whereas, for example, a puppy might be able to eat only the toe of a slipper, a child might well succeed in eating the whole shoe—which, considering the nails and everything, would not be wise.

One of the reasons why dogs are given credit for serious thinking is the formation of their eyebrows. A dog lying in front of a fire and looking up at his master may appear pathetic, disapproving, sage, or amused, according to the angle at which its eyebrows are set by nature.

It is quite possible, and even probable, that nothing at all is going on behind the eyebrows. In fact, one dog who had a great reputation for sagacity once told me in confidence that most of the time when he was supposed to be regarding a human with an age-old philosophical rumination he was really asleep behind his shaggy overhanging brows. "You could have knocked me over with a feather," he said, "when I found out that people were talking about my wisdom and suggesting running me for President."

This, of course, offers a possibility for the future of the child itself. As soon as the boy makes up his mind just what type of man he wants to be, he could buy some crêpe hair and a bottle of spirit gum and make himself a pair of eyebrows to suit the role: converging toward the nose if he wants to be a judge or savant; pointing upward from the edge of the eyes if he wants to be a worried-looking man, like a broker; elevated to his forehead if he plans on simulating surprise as a personal characteristic; and in red patches if he intends being a stage Irishman.

In this way he may be able to get away with a great deal, as his pal the dog does.

At any rate, the important thing is to get a dog for the boy and see what each can teach the other. The way things are going now with our Younger Generation, the chances are that before long the dog will be smoking, drinking gin, and wearing a soft hat pulled over one eye.

# The Rich Sardine

*Seven Droodles by Roger Price*

Droodles, explains Roger Price, are "little drawings that make a complete picture using the fewest possible lines. They are contrived doodles that you don't understand until you ask, and then it's too late to wish you hadn't."

For example, here is an example:

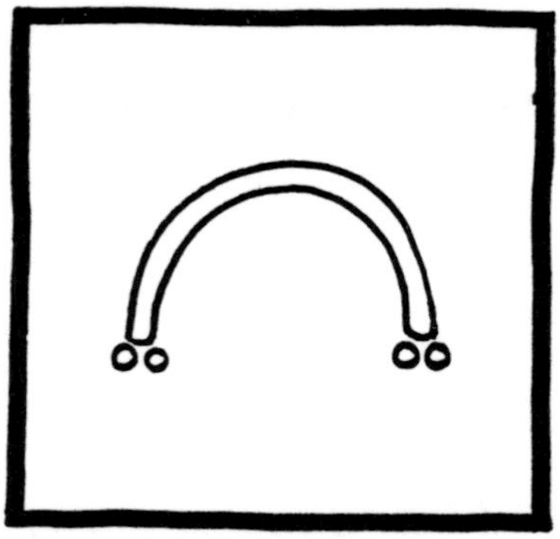

Puzzled? You shouldn't be. Obviously, this is

A WORM ROLLERSKATING

Here is example number 2:

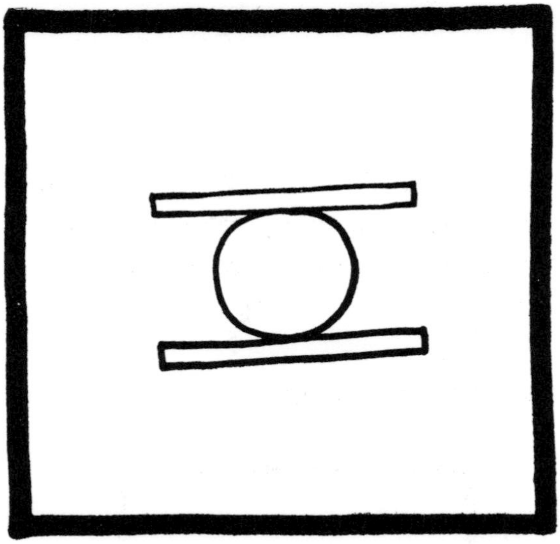

Examined closely, this can be nothing but

TOMATO SANDWICH MADE BY AN
AMATEUR TOMATO SANDWICH MAKER

Example 3:

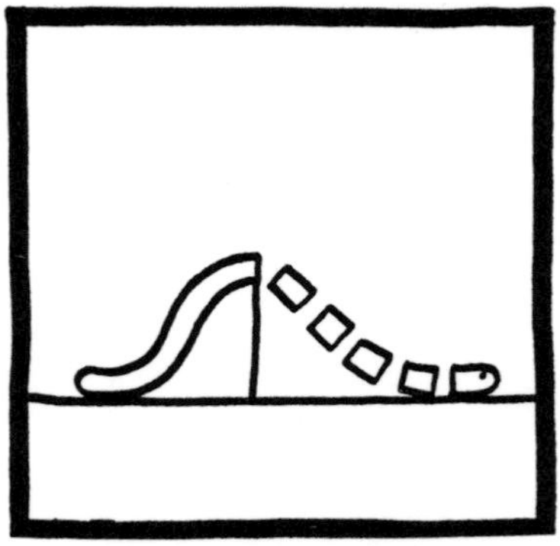

This really could be nothing else than

DETERMINED WORM
CRAWLING OVER A RAZOR BLADE

Example 4:

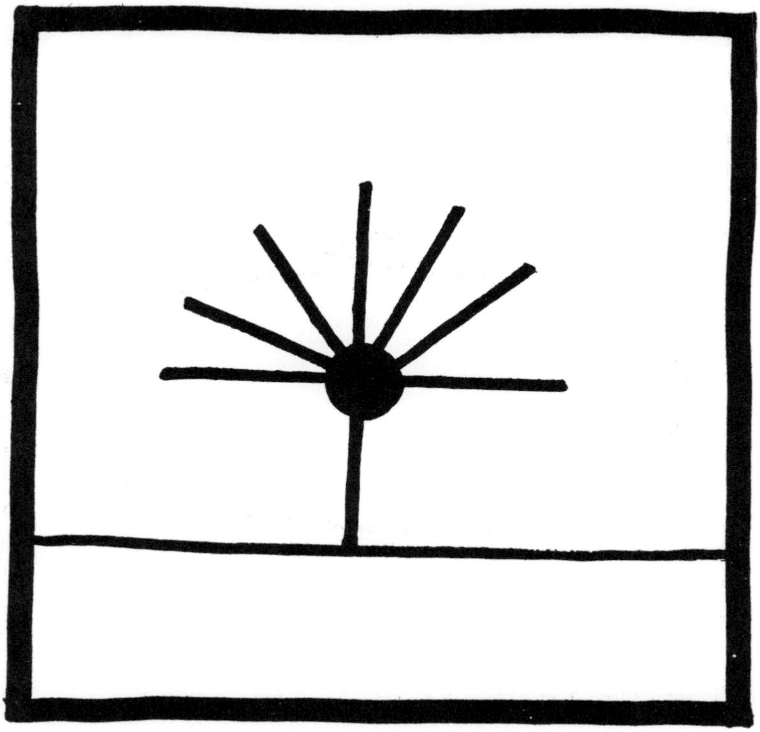

The correct title of this great work of art is

TOTAL ECLIPSE OF THE SUN ON A STICK

although two stubborn dissenters hold out, respectively, for FAMILY OF WORMS STUCK IN A CANDIED APPLE and A FRIGHTENED MOP.

Example 5:

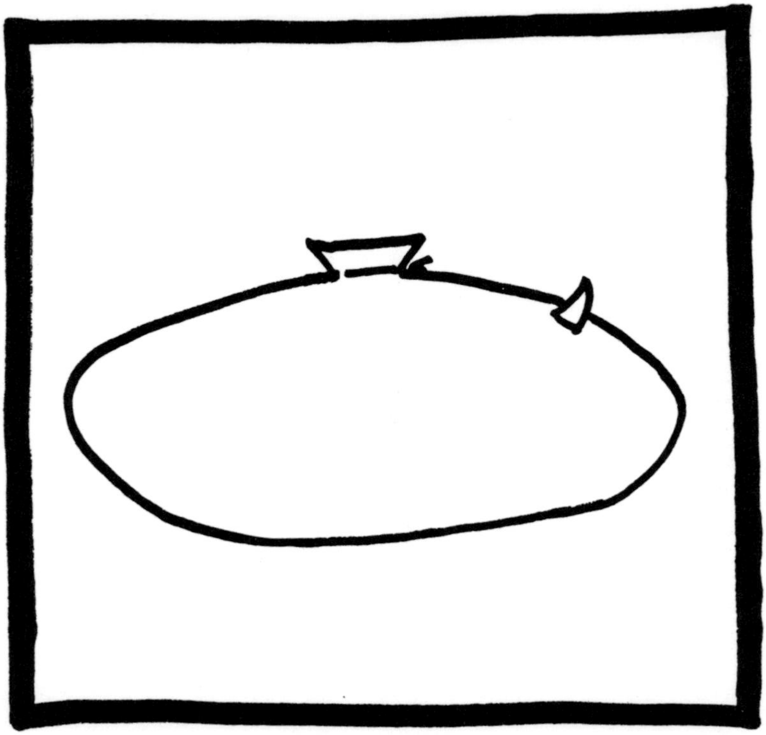

This, of course, is

A RHINOCEROS IN A PAPER BAG

although Mr. Price is apprehensive lest the suggestion of putting rhinoceroses in paper bags start a fad.

Example 6:

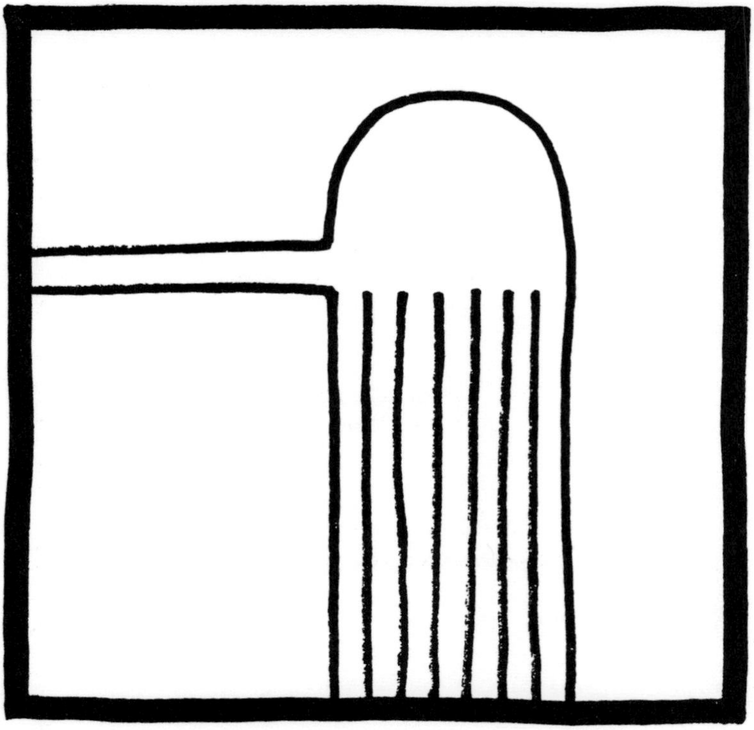

The title of this masterpiece is

OCTOPUS SIGNALING FOR A LEFT TURN

Finally, here is Example 7, which gave Roger Price the title for the book from which these droodles have been copied (with the kind permission of the maestro):

Yes, it's

THE RICH SARDINE

# Tom's Whitewash

*by Mark Twain*

Saturday morning was come, and all the summer world was bright and fresh, and brimming with life. There was a song in every heart; and if the heart was young the music issued at the lips. There was cheer in every face and a spring in every step. The locust trees were in bloom and the fragrance of the blossoms filled the air. Cardiff Hill, beyond the village and above it, was green with vegetation; and it lay just far enough away to seem a Delectable Land, dreamy, reposeful, and inviting.

Tom appeared on the sidewalk with a bucket of whitewash and a long-handled brush. He surveyed the fence, and all gladness left him and a deep melancholy settled down upon his spirit. Thirty yards of board fence nine feet high. Life to him seemed hollow, and existence but a burden. Sighing he dipped his brush and passed it along the topmost plank; repeated the operation; did it again; compared the insignificant whitewashed streak with the far-reaching continent of unwhitewashed fence, and sat down on a tree-box discouraged. Jim came skipping out at the gate with a tin pail, and singing "Buffalo Gals." Bringing water from the town pump had always been hateful work in Tom's eyes before, but now it did not strike him so. He remembered that there was company at the pump. White, mulatto, and Negro boys and girls were always there waiting their turns, resting, trading playthings, quarreling, fighting, skylarking. And he remembered that, although the pump was only a hundred and fifty yards off, Jim never got back with a bucket of water under an hour—and even then somebody generally

---

From *The Adventures of Tom Sawyer.*

had to go after him. Tom said:

"Say, Jim, I'll fetch the water if you'll whitewash some."

Jim shook his head and said:

"Can't, Marse Tom. Ole missis, she tole me I got to go an' git dis water an' not stop foolin' roun' wid anybody. She say she spec' Marse Tom gwine to ax me to whitewash, an' so she tole me go 'long an' 'tend to my own business—she 'lowed *she'd* 'tend to de whitewashin'."

"Oh, never mind what she said, Jim. That's the way she always talks. Gimme the bucket—I won't be gone only a minute. *She* won't ever know."

"Oh, I dasn't, Marse Tom. Ole missis she'd take an' tar de head off'n me. 'Deed she would."

"*She!* She never licks anybody—whacks 'em over the head with her thimble—and who cares for that, I'd like to know. She talks awful, but talk don't hurt—anyways it don't if she don't cry. Jim, I'll give you a marvel. I'll give you a white alley!"

Jim began to waver.

"White alley, Jim! And its a bully taw."

"My! Dat's a mighty gay marvel, I tell you! But Marse Tom, I's powerful 'fraid ole missis—"

"And besides, if you will I'll show you my sore toe."

Jim was only human—this attraction was too much for him. He put down his pail, took the white alley, and bent over the toe with absorbing interest while the bandage was being unwound. In another moment he was flying down the street with his pail and a tingling rear, Tom was whitewashing with vigor, and Aunt Polly was retiring from the field with a slipper in her hand and triumph in her eye.

But Tom's energy did not last. He began to think of the fun he had planned for this day, and his sorrows multiplied. Soon the free boys would come tripping along on all sorts of delicious expeditions, and they would make a world of fun of him for having to work—the very thought of it burnt him like fire. He got out his worldly wealth and examined it—bits of toys, marbles, and trash; enough to buy an exchange of *work*, maybe, but not half enough to buy so much as half an hour of pure freedom. So he returned his straitened means to his pocket and gave up the idea of trying to buy the boys. At this dark and hopeless moment an inspiration burst upon him! Nothing less than a great, magnificent inspiration.

He took up his brush and went tranquilly to work. Ben Rogers hove in sight presently—the very boy, of all boys, whose ridicule he had been dreading. Ben's gait was the hop-skip-and-jump—proof enough that his heart was light and his anticipations high. He was eating an apple, and giving a long, melodious whoop, at intervals, followed by a deep-toned ding-dong-dong, ding-dong-dong, for he was personating a steamboat. As he drew near, he slackened speed, took the middle of the street, leaned far over to starboard and rounded to ponderously and with laborious pomp and circumstance —for he was personating the *Big Missouri*, and considered himself to be drawing nine feet of water. He was boat and captain and engine bells combined, so he had to imagine himself standing on his own hurricane deck giving the orders and executing them:

"Stop her, sir! Ting-a-ling-ling!" The headway ran almost out and he drew up slowly toward the sidewalk.

"Ship up to back! Ting-a-ling-ling!" His arms straightened and stiffened down his sides.

"Set her back on the stabboard! Ting-a-ling-ling! Chow! Ch-chow-wow! Chow!" His right hand, meantime, describing stately circles—for it was representing a forty-foot wheel.

"Let her go back on the labboard! Ting-a-ling-ling! Chow-ch-chow-chow!" The left hand began to describe circles.

"Stop the stabboard! Ting-a-ling-ling! Stop the labboard! Come ahead on the stabboard! Stop her! Let your outside turn over slow! Ting-a-ling-ling! Chow-ow-ow! Get out that head line! *Lively* now! Come—out with your spring line—what're you about there! Take a turn round that stump with the bight of it! Stand by that stage, now —let her go! Done with the engines, sir! Ting-a-ling-ling! *Sh't! sh't!*

*sh't!*" (trying the gauge cocks).

Tom went on whitewashing—paid no attention to the steamboat. Ben stared a moment and then said:

"Hi-*yi! You're* up a stump, ain't you!"

No answer. Tom surveyed his last touch with the eye of an artist, then he gave his brush another gentle sweep and surveyed the result, as before. Ben ranged up alongside of him. Tom's mouth watered for the apple, but he stuck to his work. Ben said:

"Hello, old chap, you got to work, hey?"

Tom wheeled suddenly and said:

"Why, it's you, Ben! I warn't noticing."

"*Say*—I'm going in a-swimming, I am. Don't you wish you could? But of course you'd druther *work*—wouldn't you? Course you would!"

Tom contemplated the boy a bit, and said:

"What do you call work?"

"Why, ain't *that* work?"

Tom resumed his whitewashing, and answered carelessly:

"Well, maybe it is, and maybe it ain't. All I know is, it suits Tom Sawyer."

"Oh come, now, you don't mean to let on that you *like* it?"

The brush continued to move.

"Like it? Well, I don't see why I oughtn't to like it. Does a boy get a chance to whitewash a fence every day?"

That put the thing in a new light. Ben stopped nibbling his apple. Tom swept his brush daintily back and forth—stepped back to note the effect—added a touch here and there—criticized the effect again—Ben watching every move and getting more and more interested, more and more absorbed. Presently he said:

"Say, Tom let *me* whitewash a little."

Tom considered, was about to consent; but he altered his mind:

"No—no—I reckon it wouldn't hardly do, Ben. You see, Aunt Polly's awful particular about this fence—right here on the street, you know—but if it was the back fence I wouldn't mind and *she* wouldn't. Yes, she's awful particular about this fence; it's got to be done very careful; I reckon there ain't one boy in a thousand, maybe two thousand that can do it the way it's got to be done."

"No—is that so? Oh come, now—lemme just try. Only just a little—I'd let *you*, if you was me, Tom."

"Ben, I'd like to, honest Injun; but Aunt Polly—well, Jim wanted to do it, but she wouldn't let him; Sid wanted to do it, and she wouldn't let Sid. Now don't you see how I'm fixed? If you was to tackle this fence and anything was to happen to it—"

"Oh, shucks, I'll be just as careful. Now lemme try. Say—I'll give you the core of my apple."

"Well, here— No, Ben, now don't. I'm afeared—"

"I'll give you *all* of it!"

Tom gave up the brush with reluctance in his face, but alacrity in his heart. And while the late steamer *Big Missouri* worked and sweated in the sun, the retired artist sat on a barrel in the shade close by, dangled his legs, munched his apple, and planned the slaughter of more innocents. There was no lack of material; boys happened along every little while; they came to jeer, but remained to whitewash. By the time Ben was fagged out, Tom had traded the next chance to Billy Fisher for a kite, in good repair; and when *he* played out, Johnny Miller bought in for a dead rat and a string to swing it with—and so on, and so on, hour after hour. And when the middle of the afternoon came, from being a poor poverty-stricken boy in the morning, Tom was literally rolling in wealth. He had besides the things before mentioned, twelve marbles, part of a jew's-harp, a piece of blue bottle glass to look through, a spool cannon, a key that wouldn't unlock anything, a fragment of chalk, a glass stopper of a decanter, a tin soldier, a couple of tadpoles, six firecrackers, a kitten with only one eye, a brass doorknob, a dog collar—but no dog—the handle of a knife, four pieces of orange peel, and a dilapidated old window sash.

He had had a nice, good, idle time all the while—plenty of company—and the fence had three coats of whitewash on it! If he hadn't run out of whitewash, he would have bankrupted every boy in the village.

Tom said to himself that it was not such a hollow world, after all. He had discovered a great law of human action, without knowing it —namely, that in order to make a man or a boy covet a thing, it is only necessary to make the thing difficult to attain. If he had been a great and wise philosopher, like the writer of this book, he would now have comprehended that Work consists of whatever a body is *obliged* to do and that Play consists of whatever a body is not obliged to do. And this would help him to understand why constructing artificial flowers or performing on a treadmill is work, while rolling tenpins or climbing Mont Blanc is only amusement. There are wealthy gentlemen in England who drive four-horse passenger coaches twenty or thirty miles on a daily line, in the summer, because the privilege costs them considerable money; but if they were offered wages for the service, that would turn it into work and then they would resign.

The boy mused awhile over the substantial change which had taken place in his worldly circumstances, and then wended toward headquarters to report.

# Pay the Two Francs

*by Art Buchwald*

Like I said, we had this party with chopped chicken liver, turkey, ham, and various salads. But since we were giving the party with another couple, the Bernheims, we had to share with them the left-over food and also return a large, silver tray which we borrowed for the party.

So we called a taxi and carried all the food downstairs to go to the Bernheims. Every once in a while you get a taxi driver in Paris who talks to other chauffeurs. In his opinion, every driver on the road is an idiot, and also yellow. To prove it, our driver challenged every car on the Champs Elysées. All of them did prove yellow except one, another taxi driver. They both put on their brakes at the same time, avoiding a smashup, but the tray with the chopped chicken liver, ham, turkey, and salad went flying on to the floor of the taxi.

This was too much for my nerves, and I told the driver to stop the cab and let us off at the Hotel California, on the Rue de Berri. Insulted because we didn't trust his driving, he blamed us for not holding on to the tray when he had to stop to avoid an accident. He said we didn't know how to ride in a taxi. I said he didn't know how to drive one.

At the California I told my wife to get out of the cab. Then I bent down in the cab to pick up the food and the tray.

The driver said, "Pay me now."

I replied, "After I take the food out of the taxi."

He said, "I want my money right now."

---

From *Don't Forget to Write.*

I said, "You'll get it after I take the food out of the cab."

"Then we're going to the police," he said. And with the door open he put the cab into gear, and away we went, leaving my wife standing on the sidewalk.

"Nobody refuses to pay me," he said, as he drove madly in search of a police station. Unfortunately he didn't know where one was, and we kept driving around in circles. Finally he arrived not at a police station, but a police barracks where they round up Algerian terrorists.

Four policemen with submachine guns greeted us at the entrance.

It didn't seem like the place for two people who were having an argument about a taxi to get it settled, and it turned out I was right. A police captain came charging out of the barracks, furious that he was bothered. He started bawling out the taxi driver for coming there.

I was enjoying the show when he turned on me and bawled me

out for not paying the taxi driver. He demanded my identification papers and told one of the policemen to take me and the driver to a commissariat—a regular police station.

The nearest one was located in the basement of the Grand Palais, where the Paris Automobile Show is held. When we arrived the police lieutenant demanded to know what was wrong.

"Well, we had this chopped chicken liver," I said.

"You had what?" he asked in amazement.

"Chopped chicken liver in the taxi."

Everyone in the station looked up from their work.

"And we had turkey and ham and salad, and he's a lousy driver," I said.

"He won't pay me," the taxi driver said. "He had all the food on the seat, and he didn't hold on to it. Is this my fault?"

The lieutenant scratched his head. "Ça, c'est extraordinaire."

"I wanted to pay him, but I wanted to get the chicken liver out of the taxi first," I said.

"It is not true," the taxi driver said. "His wife knows it's not true."

"Where is his wife?"

"He left her standing in front of the Hotel California," I screamed.

"Calm down," the lieutenant said. "Nothing can happen to her in front of the Hotel California. Where is the chicken liver now?"

"In the bottom of the taxicab where he put it," I said accusingly.

"No," the taxi driver said, "where he let it fall."

Everyone in the police station was breaking up with laughter, and I could see I was losing the battle.

"Do you want to pay him, or not?" the lieutenant asked.

"I'll pay him after I take the food out of the taxi."

"All right," the lieutenant said. "Take the food out of the taxi and pay him."

I went back outside, and while a dozen gendarmes looked on with interest, I put the food back on the silver tray. I heard one say to another, "C'est extraordinaire. Foie de volaille haché. C'est plutôt cannibale." ("Chopped chicken liver. It's extraordinary—almost cannibal.")

I paid the taxi driver, refusing to give him a tip, and he drove off, screaming.

I didn't have the nerve to ask the lieutenant to call me another taxi, so I picked up the silver tray and, with the laughter of the police still in my ears, I walked up the Champs Elysées for five blocks.

It will be the last time we give a party with somebody else.

# Learning to Drive

*by Billy Rose*

On the way back from Mt. Kisco, my wife said, "I wish you'd learn how to drive. Every time you want something, somebody's got to stop what he's doing and chauffeur you into the village."

"Okay," I said, "if you'll play teacher."

Next morning I crawled into the car beside my wife. "Just turn this jigger over," she began, "push in this dingus, pull out this doohickey, step on this wingdoodle, press down on this thingama-bob, and you're all set to go."

"What's this gizmo?" I asked.

"The hand brake," she said. "You throw it on quickly in case of emergency."

"What happens if the brakes don't work?"

"Hit something cheap," advised my spouse.

A moment later the car went hiccuping down the road. Then for a mile it went smooth as you please. A feeling of confidence came over me, the same feeling all new drivers get just before the lights go out. I pressed down on the gas.

"The pistons seem to be knocking," I said professionally.

"Pistons nothing," said my mate. "Those are my knees."

Everything went fine until we got to the traffic light in the village. I forgot to press the hickey-madoodle on the gilhooley, and the car stalled. The lights changed from green to red, and from red back to green. A cop came over.

"What's the matter?" he asked. "Haven't we got any colors you like?"

---

From *Wine, Women, and Song.*

After switching the radio on and off, I suddenly pressed the right thing. In the order of the way it happened, I grazed the cop, skidded through the safety zone, clipped the fender on a bus, and came to rest with my bumper against a fire plug. The cop stalked over. He took a handkerchief out of his pocket and dropped it in front of the car.

"Lookit, Gene Autry," he said. "I wanna see you do that all over again, and this time pick up the handkerchief with your teeth."

My wife gave him the big smile. "He's learning to drive," she said.

"No kidding!" said the cop. "How long is this class going to last? Some other drivers would like to use this road when Sonny Boy gets through with it."

"What did I do wrong?" I asked the officer.

"Didn't you hear my whistle? Didn't you see my signal?" he demanded.

I shook my head.

The cop sighed. "I'd better go home. I don't seem to be doing much good around here."

I threw the car into reverse and backed away from the fire plug.

"If you're going to drive much," yelled the cop, "I'd have the car painted red on one side and blue on the other, so the witnesses will contradict one another."

"What kind of cops do they have in Mt. Kisco?" I asked my wife as we headed for home.

"I wouldn't know," she deadpanned. "Maybe he's Milton Berle's brother."

There are two stone posts flanking the drive which leads up to my house. I got past them without a scratch—also without the rear bumper. That did it.

Since then, I've never been behind a wheel. When we go driving, I sit in the back seat and read the Burma Shave signs. The only concession I've made to the Automotive Age is to learn how to fold a road map.

# A Turn for the Verse

MISCELLANEOUS POEMS

## The Purple Cow

*by Gelett Burgess*

I never saw a Purple Cow,
I never hope to see one,
But I can tell you, anyhow,
I'd rather see than be one!

## O I C

*Anonymous*

I'm in a 10der mood today
& feel poetic, 2;
4 fun I'll just — off a line
& send it off 2 U.

I'm sorry you've been 6 o long;
Don't B disconsol8;
But bear your ills with 42de,
& they won't seem so gr8.

# The Little Man Who Wasn't There

*by Hughes Mearns*

As I was going up the stair
I met a man who wasn't there!
He wasn't there again today!
I wish, I *wish* he'd stay away!

# Miniature

*by Richard Armour*

My day-old son is plenty scrawny,
His mouth is wide with screams, or yawny.
His ears seem larger than he's needing,
His nose is flat, his chin's receding.
His skin is very, very red
He has no hair upon his head.
And yet I'm proud as proud can be
To hear you say he looks like me.

---

"Miniature" from *For Partly Proud Parents.*

## Infant Prodigy

*by Margaret Fishback*

At six weeks Baby grinned a grin
That spread from mouth to eyes to chin.
And Doc, the smartie, had the brass
To tell me it was only gas!

## Note to a Persistent Pest

*from Groucho Marx*

Although I never yet have forgotten a face,
I'm willing to make an exception in your case.

"Infant Prodigy" from *Look Who's a Mother.*

# Habits of the Hippopotamus

*by Arthur Guiterman*

The hippopotamus is strong
And huge of head and broad of bustle;
The limbs on which he rolls along
Are big with hippopotomuscle.

He does not greatly care for sweets
Like ice cream, apple pie, or custard,
But takes to flavor what he eats
A little hippopotomustard.

The hippopotamus is true
To all his principles, and just;
He always tries his best to do
The things one hippopotomust.

He never rides in trucks or trams,
In taxicabs or omnibuses,
And so keeps out of traffic jams
And other hippopotomusses.

---

From *Gaily the Troubadour.*

## How to Tell the Wild Animals

*by Carolyn Wells*

If ever you should go by chance
To jungles in the East;
And if there should to you advance
A large and tawny beast,
If he roars at you as you're dyin'
You'll know it is the Asian Lion.

Or if some time when roaming round,
A noble wild beast greets you,
With black stripes on a yellow ground,
Just notice if he eats you.
This simple rule may help you learn
The Bengal Tiger to discern.

If strolling forth, a beast you view,
Whose hide with spots is peppered,
As soon as he has lept on you,
You'll know it is the Leopard.
'Twill do no good to roar with pain,
He'll only lep and lep again.

If when you're walking round your yard,
  You meet a creature there,
Who hugs you very, very hard,
  Be sure it is the Bear.
If you have any doubt, I guess,
He'll give you just one more caress.

Though to distinguish beasts of prey
  A novice might nonplus,
The Crocodiles you always may
  Tell from Hyenas thus:
Hyenas come with merry smiles;
But if they weep, they're Crocodiles.

The true Chameleon is small,
  A lizard sort of thing;
He hasn't any ears at all,
  And not a single wing.
If there is nothing in the tree,
'Tis the Chameleon you see.

## Eletelephony

*by Laura E. Richards*

Once there was an elephant,
Who tried to use the telephant—
No! no! I mean an elephone
Who tried to use the telephone—
(Dear me! I am not certain quite
That even now I've got it right.)

Howe'er it was, he got his trunk
Entangled in the telephunk;
The more he tried to get it free,
The louder buzzed the telephee—
(I fear I'd better drop the song
Of elephop and telephong!)

---

From *Tirra Lirra.*

## Poems in Praise of Practically Nothing

*by Samuel Hoffenstein*

You buy some flowers for your table;
You tend them tenderly as you're able.
You fetch them water from hither and thither—
What thanks do you get for it all? They wither.

You buy yourself a new suit of clothes;
The care you give it, God only knows.
The material, of course, is the very best yet;
You get it pressed and pressed and pressed yet.
You keep it free from specks so tiny—
What thanks do you get? The pants get shiny.

You leap out of bed; you start to get ready;
You dress and you dress till you feel unsteady.
Hours go by, and you're still busy
Putting on clothes, till your brain is dizzy.
Do you flinch, do you quit, do you go out naked?
The least little button, you don't forsake it.
What thanks do you get? Well, for all this mess, yet
When night comes around you've got to undress yet.

---

From the book *Poems in Praise of Practically Nothing.*

## Father William

*by Lewis Carroll*

"You are old, Father William," the young man said,
"And your hair has become very white;
And yet you incessantly stand on your head—
Do you think, at your age, it is right?"

"In my youth," Father William replied to his son,
"I feared it might injure the brain;
But now that I'm perfectly sure I have none,
Why, I do it again and again."

"You are old," said the youth, "as I mentioned before,
And have grown most uncommonly fat;
Yet you turned a back-somersault in at the door—
Pray, what is the reason for that?"

"In my youth," said the sage, as he shook his gray locks,
"I kept all my limbs very supple
By the use of this ointment—one shilling the box—
Allow me to sell you a couple?"

"You are old," said the youth, "and your jaws are too weak
For anything tougher than suet;
Yet you finished the goose, with the bones and the beak—
Pray, how did you manage to do it?"

"In my youth," said his father, "I took to the law,
And argued each case with my wife;
And the muscular strength which it gave to my jaw
Has lasted the rest of my life."

"You are old," said the youth; "one would hardly suppose
That your eye was as steady as ever;
Yet you balanced an eel on the end of your nose—
What made you so awfully clever?"

"I have answered three questions, and that is enough,"
Said his father, "don't give yourself airs!
Do you think I can listen all day to such stuff?
Be off, or I'll kick you downstairs!"

## Song of the Pop-Bottlers

*by Morris Bishop*

Pop bottles pop-bottles
In pop shops;
The pop-bottles Pop bottles
Poor Pop drops.

When Pop drops pop-bottles,
Pop-bottles plop!
Pop-bottle-tops topple!
Pop mops slop!

Stop! Pop'll drop bottle!
Stop, Pop, stop!
When Pop bottles pop-bottles,
Pop-bottles pop!

---

From *A Bowl of Bishop.*

## SIX POEMS BY OGDEN NASH

### REFLECTIONS ON BABIES

A bit of talcum
Is always walcum.

### SONG OF THE OPEN ROAD

I think that I shall never see
A billboard lovely as a tree.
Indeed, unless the billboards fall,
I'll never see a tree at all.

### THE EEL

I don't mind eels
Except at meals—
And the way they feels.

### THE LAMA

The one-L lama,
He's a priest.
The two-L llama,
He's a beast.
And I will bet
A silk pajama
There isn't any
Three-L lllama.

---

From *Verses From 1929 On.*

THE FLY

The Lord in His wisdom made the fly
And then forgot to tell us why.

THE TERMITE

Some primal termite knocked on wood
And tasted it, and found it good,
And that is why your cousin May
Fell through the parlor floor today.

## LITTLE WILLIE POEMS

The monstrous—and celebrated—"Little Willie" probably owed his original fame to Charles H. Clark, who wrote, way back in the 1870's:

Little Willie had a purple monkey climbing up
  a stick
And when he licked the paint all off, it made
  him very sick.
And in his latest hours he clasped the monkey in
  his hand,
And said goodbye to earth and went to a better land.
Oh, no more he'll shoot his sister with his little
  wooden gun,
And no more he'll twist the pussy's tail and
  make her yowl for fun.
The pussy's tail now stands up straight; the
  gun is laid aside;
The monkey doesn't jump around since Little
  Willie died.

Here are a few of the other countless outrageous activities engaged in by Little Willie since that time:

In the family drinking well
Willie pushed his sister Nell.
Said his mother, drawing water,
"It's mighty tough to raise a daughter."

Little Willie with a curse,
Threw a coffeepot at nurse.
When it struck her on the nose,
Father cheered, "How straight he throws!"

Little Willie on a farm
Fell off a horse and broke his arm
All the neighbors cried, "What fun!
Bad luck that it was only one!"

Little Willie, on one of his dashes,
Fell in the fire and was burned to ashes.
Soon the room got very chilly
But nobody liked to poke up Willie.

Willie, with a thirst for gore,
Nailed his sister to a door.
Mother said, with humor quaint,
"Willie dear! Don't scratch the paint!"

Little Willie, feeling bright,
Bought a stick of dynamite.
Curiosity seldom pays:
It rained Willie for seven days.

### TWO-LINERS

The shortest poem in the English language probably is Strickland Gillian's "Lines on the Antiquity of Fleas":

Adam
Had 'em.

Equally terse is William Benet's "Maid's Day Out."

Thurs.
Hers.

Humorist George Ade once mourned:

Last night at twelve I felt immense,
But now I feel like thirty cents.

Richard Armour made this discovery:

Shake and shake the catsup bottle:
None will come, and then a lot'll.

A man who didn't like guests posted this notice at the entrance of his driveway:

The road isn't passable;
Not even jackassable.

Begged an irritable lady at a tea party:

Please diet
In quiet.

A Seattle driver hung this sign on the back of his pick-up truck:

Spring has sprung and grass has rizz
Where last year's reckless driver is.

And a henpecked husband observed:

Women do not talk all day:
It only seems to sound that way.

OUT ON A LIMERICK

There was a young lady named Bright,
Whose speed was much faster than light.
She went out one day
In a relative way
And returned on the previous night.

There was a young lady of Niger
Who smiled as she rode on a tiger.
They returned from the ride
With the lady inside
And the smile on the face of the tiger.

---

From the book *Out on a Limerick* by Bennett Cerf.

I wish that my room had a floor;
I don't so much care for a door,
  But this walking around
  Without touching the ground
Is getting to be quite a bore!

—GELETT BURGESS

The bottle of perfume that Willie sent
Was highly displeasing to Millicent.
  Her thanks were so cold
  That they quarreled, I'm told,
Through that silly scent Willie sent Millicent.

There was an old man in a boat,
Who said, "I'm afloat! I'm afloat!"
  When they said, "No, you ain't,"
  He was ready to faint,
That unhappy old man in a boat.

—EDWARD LEAR

As a beauty I am not a star.
There are others more handsome, by far.
  But my face, I don't mind it
  For I am behind it.
It's the people in front get the jar!

—WOODROW WILSON

There was a young lady of Crete
Who was so exceedingly neat,
  When she got out of bed
  She stood on her head
To make sure of not soiling her feet.

A cat in despondency sighed
And resolved to commit suicide.
  She passed under the wheels
  Of eight automobiles
And under the ninth one she died.

There once was a lady named Harris
That nothing seemed apt to embarrass
  Till the bathsalts she shook
  In a tub that she took
Turned out to be plaster-of-Paris.

Said an envious, erudite ermine,
"There's one thing I cannot determine:
  When a dame wears my coat
  She's a person of note;
When I wear it, I'm called only vermin."

There was a sightseer named Sue
Who saw a strange beast at the zoo.
  When she asked, "Is it old?"
  She was smilingly told,
"It's not an old beast, but a gnu."

The fabulous wizard of Oz
Retired from business becoz
  What with up-to-date science,
  To most of his clients
He wasn't the wiz that he woz.

There was an old man on the Rhine
Who was asked at what hour he'd dine.
  He replied, "At eleven,
  Four, six, three, and seven.
Not to mention a quarter to nine."

There was a young man so benighted
He didn't know when he was slighted.
  He went to a party
  And ate just as hearty
As if he'd been really invited.

The fact is that Rome needed money
And, further, the Gauls got too funny.
  So they sent out some legions
  To clean up them regions.
J. Caesar? Yep, he was there, sonny.

A fellow named Crosby (not Bing)
Was asked by a hostess to sing.
  He replied, "Though it's odd,
  I can never tell 'God
Save the Weasel' from 'Pop Goes the King.' "

There was an old man of Tarentum
Who gnashed his false teeth till he bent 'em.
When they asked him the cost
Of what he had lost,
He replied, "I can't say, 'cause I rent 'em."

There was a young fellow of Perth
Who was born on the day of his birth.
He was married, they say,
On his wife's wedding day,
And he died when he quitted the earth.

A newspaper writer named Fling
Could make copy from most anything.
But the copy he wrote
Of a ten-dollar note
Was so good he is now in Sing Sing.

I'd rather have fingers than toes;
I'd rather have ears than a nose;
And as for my hair,
I'm glad it's all there.
I'll be awfully sad when it goes.

—GELETT BURGESS

When twins came, their father, Dan Dunn,
Gave "Edward" as name to each son.
When folks said, "Absurd!"
He replied, "Ain't you heard
That two Eds are better than one?"

—BERTON BRALEY

Said a foolish young lady in Wales,
"A smell of escaped gas prevails."
  Then she searched with a light
  And later that night
Was collected—in seventeen pails.

A barber who lived in Moravia
Was renowned for his fearless behavia.
  An enormous baboon
  Broke into his saloon,
But he murmured, "I'm darned if I'll shavia."

A tutor who tooted a flute
Tried to teach two young tooters to toot.
  Said the two to the tutor,
  "Is it harder to toot, or
To tutor two tooters to toot?"

—CAROLYN WELLS

A certain young chap named Bill Beebee
Was in love with a lady named Phoebe.
  "But," he said, "I must see
  What the clerical fee
Be before Phoebe be Phoebe Beebee."

In Iceland, a supple young miss
Enthused, "I think skating is bliss."
  This no more will she state
  For a slip of her skate
Left her ending up something like this.

# The Word Market

*by Norton Juster*

*In* The Phantom Tollbooth, *a boy named Milo finds his way to a strange and fascinating land. His traveling companion is Tock—a watchdog who (naturally) ticks. "The Word Market" describes one of their most entertaining adventures.*—B.C.

As they approached the market, Milo could see crowds of people pushing and shouting their way among the stalls, buying and selling, trading and bargaining. Huge wood-wheeled carts streamed into the market square from the orchards, and long caravans bound for the four corners of the kingdom made ready to leave. Sacks and boxes were piled high waiting to be delivered to the ships that sailed the Sea of Knowledge, and off to one side a group of minstrels sang songs to the delight of those either too young or too old to engage in trade. But above all the noise and tumult of the crowd could be heard the merchants' voices loudly advertising their products.

"Get your fresh-picked ifs, ands, and buts."

"Hey-yaa, hey-yaa, hey-yaa, nice ripe wheres and whens."

"Juicy, tempting words for sale."

So many words and so many people! They were from every place imaginable and some places even beyond that, and they were all busy sorting, choosing, and stuffing things into cases. As soon as one was filled, another was begun. There seemed to be no end to the bustle and activity.

Milo and Tock wandered up and down the aisles looking at the wonderful assortment of words for sale. There were short ones and easy ones for everyday use, and long and very important ones for special occasions, and even some marvelously fancy ones packed in individual gift boxes for use in royal decrees and pronouncements.

"Step right up, step right up—fancy, best-quality words right here," announced one man in a booming voice. "Step right up—ah, what can I do for you, little boy? How about a nice bagful of pronouns—or maybe you'd like our special assortment of names?"

Milo had never thought much about words before, but these looked so good that he longed to have some.

"Look, Tock," he cried, "aren't they wonderful?"

"They're fine, if you have something to say," replied Tock in a tired voice, for he was much more interested in finding a bone than in shopping for new words.

"Maybe if I buy some I can learn how to use them," said Milo eagerly as he began to pick through the words in the stall. Finally he chose three which looked particularly good to him—"quagmire," "flabbergast," and "upholstery." He had no idea what they meant, but they looked very grand and elegant.

"How much are these?" he inquired, and when the man whispered the answer he quickly put them back on the shelf and started to walk on.

"Why not take a few pounds of 'happys'?" advised the salesman. "They're much more practical—and very useful for Happy Birthday, Happy New Year, happy days, and happy-go-lucky."

"I'd like to very much," began Milo, "but—"

"Or perhaps you'd be interested in a package of 'goods'—always handy for good morning, good afternoon, good evening, and good-by," he suggested.

Milo did want to buy something, but the only money he had was the coin he needed to get back through the tollbooth, and Tock, of course, had nothing but the time.

"No, thank you," replied Milo. "We're just looking." And they continued on through the market.

As they turned down the last aisle of stalls, Milo noticed a wagon that seemed different from the rest. On its side was a small neatly lettered sign that said "DO IT YOURSELF," and inside were twenty-six bins filled with all the letters of the alphabet from A to Z.

"These are for people who like to make their own words," the man in charge informed him. "You can pick any assortment you like or buy a special box complete with all letters, punctuation marks, and a book of instructions. Here, taste an A; they're very good."

Milo nibbled carefully at the letter and discovered that it was quite sweet and delicious—just the way you'd expect an A to taste.

"I knew you'd like it," laughed the letter man, popping two G's and an R into his mouth and letting the juice drip down his chin. "A's are one of our most popular letters. All of them aren't that good," he confided in a low voice. "Take the Z, for instance—very dry and sawdusty. And the X? Why, it tastes like a trunkful of stale air. That's why people hardly ever use them. But most of the others are quite tasty. Try some more."

He gave Milo an I, which was icy and refreshing, and Tock a crisp, crunchy C.

"Most people are just too lazy to make their own words," he continued, "but it's much more fun."

"Is it difficult? I'm not much good at making words," admitted Milo, spitting the pits from a P.

"Perhaps I can be of some assistance—a-s-s-i-s-t-a-n-c-e," buzzed an unfamiliar voice, and when Milo looked up he saw an enormous bee, at least twice his size, sitting on top of the wagon.

"I am the Spelling Bee," announced the Spelling Bee. "Don't be alarmed—a-l-a-r-m-e-d."

Tock ducked under the wagon, and Milo, who was not overly fond of normal-sized bees, began to back away slowly.

"I can spell anything—a-n-y-t-h-i-n-g," he boasted, testing his wings. "Try me, try me!"

"Can you spell good-by?" suggested Milo as he continued to back away.

The bee gently lifted himself into the air and circled lazily over Milo's head.

"Perhaps—p-e-r-h-a-p-s—you are under the misapprehension—m-i-s-a-p-p-r-e-h-e-n-s-i-o-n—that I am dangerous," he said, turning a smart loop to the left. "Let me assure—a-s-s-u-r-e—you that my intentions are peaceful—p-e-a-c-e-f-u-l." And with that he settled back on top of the wagon and fanned himself with one wing. "Now," he panted, "think of the most difficult word you can and I'll spell it. Hurry up, hurry up!" And he jumped up and down impatiently.

"He looks friendly enough," thought Milo, not sure just how friendly a friendly bumblebee should be, and tried to think of a very difficult word. "Spell 'vegetable'," he suggested, for it was one that always troubled him at school.

"That is a difficult one," said the bee, winking at the letter man. "Let me see now . . . hmmmmmmm . . ." He frowned and wiped his brow and paced slowly back and forth on top of the wagon. "How much time do I have?"

"Just ten seconds," cried Milo excitedly. "Count them off, Tock."

"Oh dear, oh dear, oh dear, oh dear," the bee repeated, continuing to pace nervously. Then, just as the time ran out, he spelled as fast as he could—"v-e-g-e-t-a-b-l-e."

"Correct," shouted the letter man, and everyone cheered.

"Can you spell everything?" asked Milo admiringly.

"Just about," replied the bee with a hint of pride in his voice. "You see, years ago I was just an ordinary bee minding my own business, smelling flowers all day, and occasionally picking up part-time work in people's bonnets. Then one day I realized that I'd never amount to anything without an education and, being naturally adept at spelling, I decided that—"

"BALDERDASH!" shouted a booming voice. And from around the wagon stepped a large beetlelike insect dressed in a lavish coat, striped pants, checked vest, spats, and a high silk hat. "Let me repeat—BALDERDASH!" he shouted again, swinging his cane and clicking his heels in mid-air. "Come now, don't be ill-mannered. Isn't someone going to introduce me to the little boy?"

"This," said the bee with complete disdain, "is the Humbug. A very dislikable fellow."

"NONSENSE! Everyone loves a Humbug," shouted the Humbug. "As I was saying to the king just the other day—"

"You've never met the king," accused the bee angrily. Then, turning to Milo, he said, "Don't believe a thing this old fraud says."

"BOSH!" replied the Humbug. "We're an old and noble family, honorable to the core—Insecticus Humbugium, if I may use the

Latin. Why, we fought in the crusades with Richard the Lion Heart, crossed the Atlantic with Columbus, blazed trails with the pioneers, and today many members of the family hold prominent government positions throughout the world. History is full of Humbugs."

"A very pretty speech—s-p-e-e-c-h," sneered the bee. "Now why don't you go away? I was just advising the lad of the importance of proper spelling."

"BAH!" said the bug, putting an arm around Milo. "As soon as you learn to spell one word, they ask you to spell another. You can never catch up—so why bother? Take my advice, my boy, and forget about it. As my great-great-great-grandfather George Washington Humbug used to say—"

"You, sir," shouted the bee very excitedly, "are an impostor—i-m-p-o-s-t-o-r—who can't even spell his own name."

"A slavish concern for the composition of words is the sign of a bankrupt intellect," roared the Humbug, waving his cane furiously.

Milo didn't have any idea what this meant, but it seemed to infuriate the Spelling Bee, who flew down and knocked off the Humbug's hat with his wing.

"Be careful," shouted Milo as the bug swung his cane again, catching the bee on the foot and knocking over the box of W's.

"My foot!" shouted the bee.

"My hat!" shouted the bug—and the fight was on.

The Spelling Bee buzzed dangerously in and out of range of the Humbug's wildly swinging cane as they menaced and threatened each other, and the crowd stepped back out of danger.

"There must be some other way to—" began Milo. And then he yelled, "WATCH OUT," but it was too late.

There was a tremendous crash as the Humbug in his great fury tripped into one of the stalls, knocking it into another, then another, then another, then another, until every stall in the market place had been upset and the words lay scrambled in great confusion all over the square.

The bee, who had tangled himself in some bunting, toppled to the ground, knocking Milo over on top of him, and lay there shouting, "Help! Help! There's a little boy on me." The bug sprawled untidily on a mound of squashed letters and Tock, his alarm ringing persistently, was buried under a pile of words.

"Done what you've looked," angrily shouted one of the salesmen. He meant to say "Look what you've done," but the words had gotten so hopelessly mixed up that no one could make any sense at all.

"Do going to we what are!" complained another, as everyone set about straightening things up as well as they could.

For several minutes no one spoke an understandable sentence, which added greatly to the confusion. As soon as possible, however, the stalls were righted and the words swept into one large pile for sorting.

The Spelling Bee, who was quite upset by the whole affair, had flown off in a huff, and just as Milo got to his feet the entire police force of Dictionopolis appeared—loudly blowing his whistle.

"Now we'll get to the bottom of this," he heard someone say. "Here comes Officer Shrift."

Striding across the square was the shortest policeman Milo had ever seen. He was scarcely two feet tall and almost twice as wide, and he wore a blue uniform with white belt and gloves, a peaked cap, and a very fierce expression. He continued blowing the whistle until his face was beet red, stopping only long enough to shout, "You're guilty, you're guilty," at everyone he passed. "I've never seen anyone so guilty," he said as he reached Milo. Then, turning towards Tock, who was still ringing loudly, he said, "Turn off that dog; it's disrespectful to sound your alarm in the presence of a policeman."

He made a careful note of that in his black book and strode up and down, his hands clasped behind his back, surveying the wreckage in the market place.

"Very pretty, very pretty." He scowled. "Who's responsible for all this? Speak up or I'll arrest the lot of you."

There was a long silence. Since hardly anybody had actually seen what had happened, no one spoke.

"You," said the policeman, pointing an accusing finger at the Humbug, who was brushing himself off and straightening his hat, "you look suspicious to me."

The startled Humbug dropped his cane and nervously replied, "Let me assure you, sir, on my honor as a gentleman, that I was merely an innocent bystander, minding my own business, enjoying the stimulating sights and sounds of the world of commerce, when this young lad—"

"AHA!" interrupted Officer Shrift, making another note in his little book. "Just as I thought: boys are the cause of everything."

"Pardon me," insisted the Humbug, "but I in no way meant to imply that—"

"SILENCE!" thundered the policeman, pulling himself up to full height and glaring menacingly at the terrified bug. "And now," he continued, speaking to Milo, "where were you on the night of July 27?"

"What does that have to do with it?" asked Milo.

"It's my birthday, that's what," said the policeman as he entered "Forgot my birthday" in his little book. "Boys always forget other people's birthdays.

"You have committed the following crimes," he continued: "having a dog with an unauthorized alarm, sowing confusion, upsetting the applecart, wreaking havoc, and mincing words."

"Now see here," growled Tock angrily.

"And illegal barking," he added, frowning at the watchdog. "It's against the law to bark without using the barking meter. Are you ready to be sentenced?"

"Only a judge can sentence you," said Milo, who remembered reading that in one of his schoolbooks.

"Good point," replied the policeman, taking off his cap and putting on a long black robe. "I am also the judge. Now would you like a long or a short sentence?"

"A short one, if you please," said Milo.

"Good," said the judge, rapping his gavel three times. "I always have trouble remembering the long ones. How about 'I am'? That's the shortest sentence I know."

Everyone agreed that it was a very fair sentence, and the judge continued: "There will also be a small additional penalty of six million years in prison. Case closed," he pronounced, rapping his gavel again. "Come with me. I'll take you to the dungeon."

"Only a jailer can put you in prison," offered Milo, quoting the same book.

"Good point," said the judge, removing his robe and taking out a large bunch of keys. "I am also the jailer." And with that he led them away.

"Keep your chin up," shouted the Humbug. "Maybe they'll take a million years off for good behavior."

The heavy prison door swung back slowly and Milo and Tock followed Officer Shrift down a long dark corridor lit by only an occasional flickering candle.

"Watch the steps," advised the policeman as they started down a steep circular staircase.

The air was dank and musty—like the smell of wet blankets—and the massive stone walls were slimy to the touch. Down and down they went until they arrived at another door even heavier and stronger-looking than the first. A cobweb brushed across Milo's face and he shuddered.

"You'll find it quite pleasant here," chuckled the policeman as he slid the bolt back and pushed the door open with a screech and a squeak. "Not much company, but you can always chat with the witch."

"The witch?" trembled Milo.

"Yes, she's been here for a long time," he said, starting along another corridor.

In a few more minutes they had gone through three other doors, across a narrow footbridge, down two more corridors and another stairway, and stood finally in front of a small cell door.

"This is it," said the policeman, "All the comforts of home."

The door opened and then shut and Milo and Tock found themselves in a high vaulted cell with two tiny windows halfway up on the wall.

"See you in six million years," said Officer Shrift, and the sound of his footsteps grew fainter and fainter until it wasn't heard at all.

"It looks serious, doesn't it, Tock?" said Milo very sadly.

"It certainly does," the dog replied, sniffing around to see what their new quarters were like.

"I don't know what we're going to do for all that time; we don't even have a checker set or a box of crayons."

"Don't worry," growled Tock, raising one paw assuringly, "something will turn up. Here, wind me, will you please? I'm beginning to run down."

"You know something, Tock?" he said as he wound up the dog. "You can get in a lot of trouble mixing up words or just not knowing how to spell them. If we ever get out of here, I'm going to make sure to learn all about them."

"A very commendable ambition, young man," said a small voice from across the cell.

Milo looked up, very surprised, and noticed for the first time, in the half-light of the room, a pleasant-looking old lady quietly knitting and rocking.

"Hello," he said.

"How do you do?" she replied.

"You'd better be very careful," Milo advised. "I understand there's a witch somewhere in here."

"I am she," the old lady answered casually, and pulled her shawl a little closer around her shoulders.

Milo jumped back in fright and quickly grabbed Tock to make sure that his alarm didn't go off—for he knew how much witches hate loud noises.

"Don't be frightened," she laughed. "I'm not a witch—I'm a Which."

"Oh," said Milo, because he couldn't think of anything else to say.

"I'm Faintly Macabre, the not-so-wicked Which," she continued, "and I'm certainly not going to harm you."

"What's a Which?" asked Milo, releasing Tock and stepping a little closer.

"Well," said the old lady, just as a rat scurried across her foot, "I am the king's great aunt. For years and years I was in charge of choosing which words were to be used for all occasions, which ones to say and which ones not to say, which ones to write and which ones not to write. As you can well imagine, with all the thousands to choose from, it was a most important and responsible job. I was given the title of 'Official Which,' which made me very proud and happy.

"At first I did my best to make sure that only the most proper and fitting words were used. Everything was said clearly and simply and no words were wasted. I had signs posted all over the palace and market place which said: BREVITY IS THE SOUL OF WIT.

"But power corrupts, and soon I grew miserly and chose fewer and fewer words, trying to keep as many as possible for myself. I had new signs posted which said: AN ILL-CHOSEN WORD IS THE FOOL'S MESSENGER.

"Soon sales began to fall off in the market. The people were afraid to buy as many words as before, and hard times came to the kingdom. But still I grew more and more miserly. Soon there were so few words chosen that hardly anything could be said, and even casual conversation became difficult. Again I had new signs posted, which said: SPEAK FITLY OR BE SILENT WISELY.

"And finally I had even these replaced by ones which read simply: SILENCE IS GOLDEN.

"All talk stopped. No words were sold, the market place closed down, and the people grew poor and disconsolate. When the king saw what had happened, he became furious and had me cast into this dungeon where you see me now, an older and wiser woman.

"That was all many years ago," she continued, "but they never appointed a new Which, and that explains why today people use as many words as they can and think themselves very wise for doing so. For always remember that while it is wrong to use too few, it is often far worse to use too many."

When she had finished, she sighed deeply, patted Milo gently on the shoulder, and began knitting once again.

"And have you been down here ever since then?" asked Milo sympathetically.

"Yes," she said sadly. "Most people have forgotten me entirely, or remember me wrongly as a witch not a Which. But it matters not, it matters not," she went on unhappily, "for they are equally frightened of both."

"I don't think you're frightening," said Milo, and Tock wagged his tail in agreement.

"I thank you very much," said Faintly Macabre. "You may call me Aunt Faintly. Here, have a punctuation mark." And she held out a box of sugar-coated question marks, periods, commas, and exclamation points. "That's all I get to eat now."

"Well, when I get out of here, I'm going to help you," Milo declared forcefully.

"I'm afraid there's not much a little boy and a dog can do," she said, "but never you mind; it's not so bad. I've grown quite used to it here. But you must be going or else you'll waste the whole day."

"Oh, we're here for six million years," sighed Milo, "and I don't see any way to escape."

"Nonsense," scolded the Which, "you mustn't take Officer Shrift so seriously. He loves to put people in prison, but he doesn't care about keeping them there. Now just press the button in the wall and be on your way."

Milo pressed the button and a door swung open, letting in a shaft of brilliant sunshine.

"Good-by; come again," shouted the Which as they stepped outside and the door slammed shut.

# The Night the Bed Fell

*by James Thurber*

I suppose that the high-water mark of my youth in Columbus, Ohio, was the night the bed fell on my father. It makes a better recitation (unless, as some friends of mine have said, one has heard it five or six times) than it does a piece of writing, for it is almost necessary to throw furniture around, shake doors, and bark like a dog, to lend the proper atmosphere and verisimilitude to what is admittedly a somewhat incredible tale. Still, it did take place.

It happened, then, that my father had decided to sleep in the attic one night, to be away where he could think. My mother opposed the notion strongly because, she said, the old wooden bed

---

From *The New Yorker.*

up there was unsafe: it was wobbly and the heavy headboard would crash down on father's head in case the bed fell, and kill him. There was no dissuading him, however, and at a quarter past ten he closed the attic door behind him and went up the narrow twisting stairs. We later heard ominous creakings as he crawled into bed. Grandfather, who usually slept in the attic bed when he was with us, had disappeared some days before. (On these occasions he was usually gone six or eight days and returned growling and out of temper, with the news that the federal Union was run by a passel of blockheads and that the Army of the Potomac didn't have any more chance than a fiddler's bitch.)

We had visiting us at this time a nervous first cousin of mine named Briggs Beall, who believed that he was likely to cease breathing when he was asleep. It was his feeling that if he were not awakened every hour during the night, he might die of suffocation. He had been accustomed to setting an alarm clock to ring at intervals until morning, but I persuaded him to abandon this. He slept in my room and I told him that I was such a light sleeper that if anybody quit breathing in the same room with me, I would wake instantly. He tested me the first night—which I had suspected he would—by holding his breath after my regular breathing had convinced him I was asleep. I was not asleep, however, and called to him. This seemed to allay his fears a little, but he took the precaution of putting a glass of spirits of camphor on a little table at the head of his bed. In case I didn't arouse him until he was almost gone, he said, he would sniff the camphor, a powerful reviver.

Briggs was not the only member of his family who had his crotchets. Old Aunt Melissa Beall (who could whistle like a man, with two fingers in her mouth) suffered under the premonition that she was destined to die on South High Street, because she had been born on South High Street and married on South High Street.

Then there was Aunt Sarah Shoaf, who never went to bed at night without the fear that a burglar was going to get in and blow chloroform under her door through a tube. To avert this calamity—

for she was in greater dread of anesthetics than of losing her household goods—she always piled her money, silverware, and other valuables in a neat stack just outside her bedroom with a note reading: "This is all I have. Please take it and do not use your chloroform, as this is all I have."

Aunt Gracie Shoaf also had a burglar phobia, but she met it with more fortitude. She was confident that burglars had been getting into her house every night for forty years. The fact that she never missed anything was to her no proof to the contrary. She always claimed that she scared them off before they could take anything, by throwing shoes down the hallway. When she went to bed she piled, where she could get at them handily, all the shoes there were about her house. Five minutes after she had turned off the light, she would sit up in bed and say "Hark!" Her husband, who had learned to ignore the whole situation as long ago as 1903, would either be sound asleep or pretend to be sound asleep. In either case he would not respond to her tugging and pulling, so that presently she would arise, tiptoe to the door, open it slightly and heave a shoe down the hall in one direction and its mate down the hall in the other direction. Some nights she threw them all, some nights only a couple of pair.

But I am straying from the remarkable incidents that took place during the night that the bed fell on father. By midnight we were all in bed. The layout of the rooms and the disposition of their occupants is important to an understanding of what later occurred. In the front room upstairs (just under father's attic bedroom) were my mother and my brother, Herman, who sometimes sang in his sleep, usually "Marching Through Georgia" or "Onward, Christian Soldiers." Briggs Beall and myself were in a room adjoining this one. My brother Roy was in a room across the hall from ours. Our bull terrier, Rex, slept in the hall.

My bed was an army cot, one of those affairs which are made wide enough to sleep on comfortably only by putting up, flat with the middle section, the two sides which ordinarily hang down like the sideboards of a drop-leaf table. When these sides are up, it is perilous to roll too far toward the edge, for then the cot is likely to tip completely over, bringing the whole bed down on top of one with a tremendous banging crash. This, in fact, is precisely what happened, about two o'clock in the morning. (It was my mother who, in recalling the scene later, first referred to it as "the night the bed fell on your father.")

Always a deep sleeper, slow to arouse (I had lied to Briggs), I was at first unconscious of what had happened when the iron cot rolled me onto the floor and toppled over on me. It left me still warmly bundled up and unhurt, for the bed rested above me like a canopy. Hence I did not wake up, only reached the edge of consciousness and went back. The racket, however, instantly awakened my mother, in the next room, who came to the immediate conclusion that her worst dread was realized: the big wooden bed upstairs had fallen on father. She therefore screamed, "Let's go to your poor father!" It was this shout, rather than the noise of my cot falling, that awakened my brother Herman, in the same room with her. He thought that mother had become, for no apparent reason, hysterical. "You're all right, mamma!" he shouted, trying to calm her. They exchanged shout for shout for perhaps ten seconds: "Let's go to your poor father!" and "You're all right!" That woke up Briggs. By this time I was conscious of what was going on, in a vague way, but did not yet realize that I was under my bed instead of on it. Briggs, awakening in the midst of loud shouts of fear and apprehension, came to the quick conclusion that he was suffocating and that we were all trying to "bring him out." With a low moan, he grasped the glass of camphor at the head of his bed and instead of sniffing it poured it over himself. The room reeked of camphor. "Ugf, ahfg!" choked Briggs, like a drowning man, for he had almost succeeded in stopping his breath under the deluge of pungent spirits. He leaped out of bed and groped toward the open window, but he came up against one that was closed. With his hand, he beat out the glass, and I could hear it crash and tinkle in the alleyway below. It was at this juncture that I, in trying to get up, had the uncanny sensation of feeling my bed above me! Foggy with sleep, I now suspected, in my turn, that the whole uproar was being made in a frantic endeavor to extricate me from what must be an unheard-of and perilous situation. "Get me out of this!" I bawled. "Get me out!" I think I had the nightmarish belief that I was entombed in a mine. "Gugh!" gasped Briggs, floundering in his camphor.

By this time my mother, still shouting, pursued by Herman, still shouting, was trying to open the door to the attic, in order to go up and get my father's body out of the wreckage. The door was stuck, however, and wouldn't yield. Her frantic pulls on it only added to the general banging and confusion. Roy and the dog were now up, the one shouting questions, the other barking.

Father, farthest away and soundest sleeper of all, had by this time been awakened by the battering on the attic door. He decided that the house was on fire. "I'm coming, I'm coming!" he wailed in a slow, sleepy voice—it took him many minutes to regain full consciousness. My mother, still believing he was caught under the bed, detected in his "I'm coming!" the mournful, resigned note of one who is preparing to meet his Maker. "He's dying!" she shouted.

"I'm all right!" Briggs yelled, to reassure her. "I'm all right!" He still believed that it was his own closeness to death that was worrying mother. I found at last the light switch in my room, unlocked the door, and Briggs and I joined the others at the attic door. The dog, who never did like Briggs, jumped for him—assuming that he was the culprit in whatever was going on—and Roy had to throw Rex and hold him. We could hear father crawling out of bed upstairs. Roy pulled the attic door open, with a mighty jerk, and father came down the stairs, sleepy and irritable but safe and sound. My mother began to weep when she saw him. Rex began to howl. "What in the name of God is going on here?" asked father.

The situation was finally put together like a gigantic jigsaw puzzle. Father caught a cold from prowling around in his bare feet but there were no other bad results. "I'm glad," said mother, who always looked on the bright side of things, "that your grandfather wasn't here."

# The Face Is Familiar But——

*by Max Shulman*

You can never tell. Citizens, you can never tell. Take the week end of May 18. From all indications it was going to be a dreamboat. Saturday night was the fraternity formal, and Sunday night Petey Burch was taking me to the Dr. Askit quiz broadcast. Every prospect pleased.

At 7:30 Saturday night I got into my rented tux and picked up my rented car. At 8:30 I called for my date and was told that she had come down with the measles at 7:30. So I shugged my rented shoulders, got into my rented car, and went to the dance alone.

I had taken my place in the stag line when Petey Burch rushed up to me, his face flushed with excitement. He waved a letter at me. "I've got it!" he cried. "Here's a letter from my parents saying I can join the Navy." Petey, like me, was seventeen years old and needed permission from home to enlist.

"That's swell, Petey," I said. "I've got some news too. My date has the measles."

"Tough," he said sympathetically. Then he suddenly got more excited than ever and hollered: "No! No, that's perfect. Listen, Dobie, the recruiting station is still open. I can go right down and enlist now."

"But what about the dance? What about your date?"

"The Navy," said Petey, snapping to attention, "needs men now. Every minute counts. How can I think of staying at a dance when there's a war to be won? I've got to get out of here, Dobie. I owe it to the boys Over There."

---

From *The Many Loves of Dobie Gillis.*

"What are you going to tell your date?"

"That's where you come in, Dobie. You take my girl; I go catch a bus. I won't tell her anything. I'll just disappear and you explain it to her later."

"Won't she mind?"

"I suppose she will, but it doesn't really matter. This is the first date I've ever had with her and I'll probably never see her again." He set his jaw. "God knows when I'll be coming back from Over There."

"I understand," I said simply.

"Thanks, old man," he said simply.

We shook hands.

"By the way," I said, "what about those two tickets you've got for the Dr. Askit broadcast tomorrow night?"

"They're yours," he said, handing them to me.

"Thanks, old man," I said simply.

"Here comes my date now," Petey said, pointing at the powder-room door. I took one look at her and knew what a patriot he must be to run out on a smooth operator like that. She was strictly on the side of angels.

"Where'd you find her?" I drooled.

"Just met her the other night. She's new around here. Now. I'll introduce you and you dance with her while I make my get-away."

"Solid," I agreed.

She walked over to us, making pink-taffeta noises. The timing was perfect. The orchestra was tuning up for the first number just as she reached us.

"Hi," said Petey. "I want you to meet a friend of mine. Dobie Gillis, this is——"

At that instant the orchestra started to play and I didn't catch her name. And no wonder. The orchestra was led by a trumpeter who had a delusion that good trumpeting and loud trumpeting are the same thing. Between him and Harry James, he figured, were only a few hundred decibels of volume. Every time he played he narrowed the gap.

"Excuse me," shouted Petey, and left.

"Dance?" I yelled.

"What?" she screamed.

I made dancing motions and she nodded. We moved out on the floor. I tried to tell her while we were dancing that I hadn't caught her name, but it was impossible. The trumpeter, feeling himself gaining on Harry James, was pursuing his advantage hard. At last there came a short trumpet break, and I made a determined stab at it.

"I don't like to seem dull," I said to the girl, "but when Petey

introduced us, I didn't catch your———"

But the trumpeter was back on the job, stronger than ever after his little rest. The rest of the song made the "Anvil Chorus" sound like a lullaby. I gave up then, and we just danced.

Came the intermission and I tried again. "I know this is going to sound silly, but when we were intro———"

"I wonder where Petey is," she interrupted. "He's been gone an awfully long time."

"Oh, not so long really. Well, as I was saying, it makes me feel foolish to ask, but I didn't———"

"It has, too, been a long time. I think that's an awfully funny way for a boy to act when he takes a girl out for the first time. Where do you suppose he is?"

"Oh, I don't know. Probably just—oh well, I suppose I might as well tell you now." So I told her.

She bit her lip. "Dobie," she quavered, "will you please take me home?"

"Home? It's so early."

"Please, Dobie."

Seventeen years of experience had taught me not to argue with a woman whose eyes are full of tears. I went and got my Driv-Ur-Self limousine, packed her into it, and started off.

"I—live—at—2123—Fremont—Avenue," she wailed.

"There, there," I cooed. "Try to look at it this way. The Navy needs men now. The longer he stayed around the dance tonight, the longer the war would last. Believe me, if my parents would sign a letter for me, I'd be Over There plenty quick, believe me."

"You mean," she wept, "that you would run off and stand up a girl at a formal affair?"

"Well," I said, "maybe not that. I mean I would hardly run out on a girl like you." I took her hand. "A girl so beautiful and lovely and pretty."

She smiled through tears. "You're sweet, Dobie."

"Oh, pshaw," I pshawed. "Say, I've got a couple of tickets to the Dr. Askit quiz broadcast tomorrow night. How about it?"

"Oh, Dobie, I'd love to. Only I don't know if Daddy will let me. He wants me to stay in and study tomorrow night. But I'll see what I can do. You call me."

"All right," I said, "but first there's something you have to tell me." I turned to her. "Now, please don't think that I'm a jerk, but it wasn't my fault. When Petey introduced us, I didn't——"

At this point I ran into the rear end of a bus. There followed a period of unpleasantness with the bus driver, during which I got a pithy lecture on traffic regulations. I don't know what he had to be sore about. His bus wasn't even nicked. The radiator grill of my car, on the other hand, was a total loss.

And when I got back in the car, there was more grief. The sudden stop had thrown the girl against the windshield head first, and her hat, a little straw number with birds, bees, flowers, and a patch of real grass, was now a heap of rubble. She howled all the way home.

"I'm afraid this evening hasn't been much fun," I said truly as I walked her to her door.

"I'm sorry, Dobie," she sniffled. "I'm sorry all this had to happen to you. You've been so nice to me."

"Oh, it's nothing any young American wouldn't have done," I said.

"You've been very sweet," she repeated. "I hope we'll get to be very good friends."

"Oh, we will. We certainly will."

She was putting her key in the lock.

"Just one more thing," I said. "Before you go in, there's something I have to know——"

"Of course," she said. "I asked you to call and didn't give you my number. It's Kenwood 6817."

"No," I said, "it's not that. I mean yes, I wanted that too. But there's another thing."

"Certainly, Dobie," she whispered and kissed me quickly. Then the door was closed behind her.

"Nuts," I mumbled, got into the car, returned it to the Driv-Ur-Self service, where I left a month's allowance to pay for the broken grille, and went back to the fraternity house.

A few of the guys were sitting in the living room. "Hi, Dobie," called one. "How'd you come out with that smooth operator? Petey sure picked the right night to run off and join the Navy, eh?"

"Oh, she was fine," I answered. "Say, do any of you fellows know her name?"

"No, you lucky dog. She's all yours. Petey just met her this week and you're the only one he introduced her to. No competition. You lucky dog."

"Yeah, sure," I said. "Lucky dog." And I went upstairs to bed.

It was a troubled night, but I had a headful of plans when I got up in the morning. After all, the problem wasn't so difficult. Finding out a girl's name should be no task for a college freshman, a crossword-puzzle expert, and the senior-class poet of the Salmon P. Chase High School, Blue Earth, Minnesota.

First I picked up the phone and dialed the operator. "Hello," I said, "I'd like to find out the name of the people who live at 2123 Fremont Avenue. The number is Kenwood 6817."

"I'm sorry. We're not allowed to give out that information."

I hung up. Then I tried plan No. 2. I dialed Kenwood 6817. A gruff male voice answered, "Hello."

"Hello," I said, "Who is this?"

"Who is *this*?" he said.

"This is Dobie Gillis. Who is this?"

"Who did you wish to speak to?"

Clearly, I was getting nowhere. I hung up.

Then I went and knocked on the door of Ed Beasley's room. Ed was a new pledge of the fraternity, and he was part of my third plan. He opened the door. "Enter, master," he said in the manner required of new pledges.

"Varlet," I said, "I have a task for you. Take yon telephone book and look through it until you find the name of the people who have telephone number Kenwood 6817."

"But, master——" protested Ed.

"I have spoken," I said sharply and walked off briskly, rubbing my palms.

In ten minutes Ed was in my room with Roger Goodhue, the president of the fraternity. "Dobie," said Roger, "you are acquainted with the university policy regarding the hazing of pledges."

"Hazing?"

"You know very well that hazing was outlawed this year by the Dean of Student Affairs. And yet you go right ahead and haze poor

Ed. Do you think more of your own amusement than the good of the fraternity? Do you know that if Ed had gone to the dean instead of me we would have had our charter taken away? I am going to insist on an apology right here and now."

Ed got his apology and walked off briskly, rubbing his palms.

"We'll have no more of that," said Roger, and he left too.

I took the phone book myself and spent four blinding hours looking for Kenwood 6817. Then I remembered that Petey had said the girl was new around here. The phone book was six months old; obviously her number would not be listed until a new edition was out.

The only course left to me was to try calling the number again in the hope that she would answer the phone herself. This time I was lucky. It was her voice.

"Hello," I cried, "who is this?"

"Why, it's Dobie Gillis," she said. "Daddy said you called before. Why didn't you ask to talk to me?"

"We were cut off," I said.

"About tonight: I can go to the broadcast with you. I told Daddy we were going to the library to study. So be sure you tell the same story when you get here. I better hang up now. I hear Daddy coming downstairs. See you at eight. 'Bye."

"Goodbye," I said.

And goodbye to some lovely ideas. But I was far from licked. When I drove up to her house at eight in a car I had borrowed from a fraternity brother (I wisely decided not to try the Driv-Ur-Self people again), I still had a few aces up my sleeve. It was now a matter of pride with me. I thought of the day I had recited the senior-class poem at Salmon P. Chase High School and I said to myself, "By George, a man who could do that can find a simple girl's name, by George." And I wasn't going to be stupid about it either. I wasn't going to just ask her. After all this trouble, I was going to be sly about it. Sly, see?

I walked up to the porch, looking carefully for some marker with the family name on it. There was nothing. Even on the mailbox there was no name.

But in the mailbox was a letter! Quickly I scooped it out of the box, just in time to be confronted by a large, hostile man framed in a suddenly open doorway.

"And what, pray, are you doing in our mailbox?" he asked with dangerous calmness.

"I'm Dobie Gillis," I squeaked. "I'm here to call on your daughter. I just saw the mail in the box and thought I'd bring it in to you." I gave him a greenish smile.

"So you're the one who hung up on me this afternoon." He placed a very firm hand on my shoulder. "Come inside, please, young man," he said.

The girl was sitting in the living room. "Do you know this fellow?" asked her father.

"Of course, Daddy. That's Dobie Gillis, the boy who is going to take me over to the library to study tonight. Dobie, this my father."

"How do you do, Mr. Zzzzzm," I mumbled.

"What?" he said.

"Well, we better run along," I said, taking the girl's hand.

"Just a moment, young man. I'd like to ask you a few things," said her father.

"Can't wait," I chirped. "Every minute counts. Stitch in time saves nine. Starve a cold and stuff a fever. Spare the rod and spoil the child." Meanwhile I was pulling the girl closer and closer to the door. "A penny saved is a penny earned," I said and got her out on the porch.

"It's such a nice night," I cried. "Let's run to the car." I had her in the car and the car in low and picking up speed fast before she could say a word.

"Dobie, you've been acting awfully strange tonight," she said with perfect justification. "I think I want to go home."

"Oh no, no, no. Not that. I'm just excited about our first real date, that's all."

"Sometimes you're so strange, and then sometimes you're so sweet. I can't figure you out."

"I'm a complex type," I admitted. And then I went to work. "How do you spell your name?" I asked.

"Just the way it sounds. What did you think?"

"Oh, I thought so. I just was wondering." I rang up a "No Sale" and started again. "Names are my hobby," I confessed. "Just before I came to get you tonight I was looking through a dictionary of names. Do you know, for instance, that Dorothy means 'gift of God'?"

"No. Really?"

"Yes. And Beatrice means 'making happy,' and Gertrude means 'spear maiden.' "

"Wonderful. Do you know any more?"

"Thousands," I said. "Abigail means 'my father's joy,' Margaret means 'a pearl,' Phyllis means 'a green bough,' and Beulah means 'she who is to be married.' " My eyes narrowed craftily; I was about to spring the trap. "Do you know what your name means?"

"Sure," she said. "It doesn't mean anything. I looked it up once, and it just said that it was from the Hebrew and didn't mean anything."

We were in front of the broadcasting studio. "Curses," I cursed and parked the car.

We went inside and were given tickets to hold. In a moment Dr. Askit took the stage and the broadcast began. "Everyone who came in here tonight was given a ticket," said Dr. Askit. "Each ticket has a number. I will now draw numbers out of this fishbowl here and call them off. If your number is called, please come up on the stage and be a contestant." He reached into the fishbowl. "The first number is 174. Will the person holding 174 please come up here?"

"That's you," said the girl excitedly.

I thought fast. If I went upon the stage, I had a chance to win $64. Not a very good chance, because I'm not very bright about these things. But if I gave the girl my ticket and had her go up, Dr.

Askit would make her give him her name and I would know what it was and all this nonsense would be over. It was the answer to my problem. "You go," I told her. "Take my ticket and go."

"But, Dobie——"

"Go ahead." I pushed her out in the aisle.

"And here comes a charming young lady," said Dr. Askit. He helped her to the microphone. "A very lucky young lady, I might add. Miss, do you know what you are?"

"What?"

"You are the ten thousandth contestant that has appeared on the Dr. Askit quiz program. And do you know what I am going to do in honor of this occasion?"

"What?"

"I am going to pay you ten times as much as I ordinarily pay contestants. Instead of a $64 maximum, you have a chance to win $640!"

"I may have to pay $640 to learn this girl's name," I thought, and waves of blackness passed before my eyes.

"Now," said Dr. Askit, "what would you like to talk about? Here is a list of subjects."

Without hesitation she said, "Number Six. The meaning of names of girls."

I tore two handfuls of upholstery from my seat.

"The first one is Dorothy," said Dr. Askit.

"Gift of God," replied the girl.

"Right! You now have $10. Would you like to try for $20? All right? The next one is Beatrice."

Two real tears ran down my cheeks. The woman sitting next to me moved over one seat.

"Making happy," said the girl.

"Absolutely correct!" crowed Dr. Askit. "Now would you care to try for $40?"

"You'll be sorry!" sang someone.

"Like hell she will!" I hollered.

"I'll try," she said.

"Gertrude," said Dr. Askit.

"Forty dollars," I mourned silently. A sports coat. A good rod and reel. A new radiator grille for a Driv-Ur-Self car.

"Spear maiden," said the girl.

"Wonderful! There's no stopping this young lady tonight. How about the $80 question? Yes? All right. Abigail. Think now. This is a toughie."

"Oh, that's easy. My father's joy."

"Easy, she said. Easy. Go ahead," I wept, as I pommeled the arm of my seat, "rub it in. Easy!"

"You certainly know your names," said Dr. Askit admiringly. "What do you say to the $160 question? All right? Margaret."

"A pearl."

The usher came over to my seat and asked if anything was wrong. I shook my head mutely. "Are you sure?" he said. I nodded. He left, but kept looking at me.

"In all my years in radio," said Dr. Askit, "I have never known such a contestant. The next question, my dear, is for $320. Will you try?"

"Shoot," she said gaily.

"Phyllis."

"A green bough."

"Right! Correct! Absolutely correct!"

Two ushers were beside me now. "I see them epileptics before," one whispered to the other. "We better get him out of here."

"Go away," I croaked, flecking everyone near me with light foam.

"Now," said Dr. Askit, "will you take the big chance? The $640 question?"

She gulped and nodded.

"For $640—Beulah."

"She who is to be married," she said.

The ushers were tugging at my sleeves.

"And the lady wins $640! Congratulations! And now, may I ask you your name?"

"Come quietly, bud," said the ushers to me. "Please don't make us use no force."

"Great balls of fire, don't make me go now!" I cried. "Not now! I paid $640 to hear this."

"My name," she said, "is Mary Brown."

"You were sweet," she said to me as we drove home, "to let me go up there tonight instead of you."

"Think nothing of it, Mary Brown," I said bitterly.

She threw back her head and laughed. "You're so funny, Dobie. I think I like you more than any boy I've ever met."

"Well, that's something to be thankful for, Mary Brown," I replied.

She laughed some more. Then she leaned over and kissed my cheek. "Oh, Dobie, you're marvelous."

So Mary Brown kissed me and thought I was marvelous. Well, that was just dandy.

"Marvelous," she repeated and kissed me again.

"Thank you, Mary Brown," I said.

No use being bitter about it. After all, $640 wasn't all the money in the world. Not quite, anyhow. I had Mary Brown, now. Maybe I could learn to love her after a while. She looked easy enough to love. Maybe someday we would get married. Maybe there would even be a dowry. A large dowry. About $640.

I felt a little better. But just a little.

I parked in front of her house. "I'll never forget this evening as long as I live," she said as we walked to the porch.

"Nor I, Mary Brown," I said truthfully.

She giggled. She put her key in the front door. "Would you like to come in, Dobie—dear?"

"No thanks, Mary Brown. I have a feeling your father doesn't care for me." Then it dawned on me. "Look!" I cried. "Your father.

You told him you were at the library tonight. What if he was listening to the radio tonight and heard you on the Dr. Askit program?"

"Oh, don't worry. People's voices sound different over the radio."

"But the name! You gave your name!"

She looked at me curiously. "Are you kiddin'? You know very well I didn't give my right name. . . . DOBIE! WHY ARE YOU BEATING YOUR HEAD AGAINST THE WALL?"

# Practice Mission

*by Mac Hyman*

*Ever since* No Time for Sergeants *was published in 1954, readers old and young have been laughing over the misadventures of Mac Hyman's blundering, well-meaning hillbilly, Will Stockdale—first in book form, then on Broadway, in television, and on the screen. There follows one of the hilarious highlights of Stockdale's wild and woolly military career.*—B.C.

After we got assigned to gunnery, me and Ben both got to be airmans-third-class which means you wear a stripe on your arm, only we didnt get to wear it long because of this Captain that was in charge of our crew in transition. He was the pilot of the plane and was always real particular, wanting you to wear neckties and such most of the time, which I didnt care nothing about. Anyhow, he stopped me and Ben up town one day and I didnt have my tie on, and we had a few words about that when I tried to explain to him how it was, which I found out later I warnt supposed to do—Ben said all I was supposed to do was stand there and say "No excuse, sir," which sounded like a kind of foolish way to talk to a man—so one thing led to another and we was recruits again; and besides that he changed us off his crew and put us in another crew. And Ben didnt like that too much because he said we was now on the *sorriest* crew on the base. He said everybody knowed it was the worst crew there, but I didnt think so myself because I got along with them pretty good. They was real easygoing compared to the other one; it didnt make much difference with them whether you showed up for a mission or not. Lieutenant Bridges was the pilot and he was a Reserve and was the only one of the officers I knowed much at first because the planes was so monstrously big and because we flew in the back and they flew in the front so that we didnt see much of the others, and didnt know them usually when we did. But Lieutenant Bridges was a mighty easygoing fellow and didnt care much what you done; he went around most of the time with his eyes about half-opened and half-closed, just kind of dragging himself around like he was walking in his sleep, only he just seemed that way, I think; he warnt really asleep but probably only half drunk, even though it was kind of hard to tell the difference most of the time. And as far as I was concerned, I had ruther been on his crew than the first one because he was so easy to work for. If you took it in your head you didnt want to go on a mission, he never would notice you warnt there nohow. I mean like this one fellow we had; he didnt fly hardly any and one day when he come out to the plane, Lieutenant Bridges didnt remember him and wouldnt let him fly with us until he went back to Operations and got a card showing he was supposed to be on our crew.

Anyhow, Sergeant King got back to being a sergeant again by that time and had got himself a job in the Orderly Room, and me and Ben hung around a good bit, not doing much but going on practice missions, and Ben finally quit worrying about losing his stripe, and we had a right nice time. Ben still didn't like the crew much—he was mighty disappointed in them most of the time and said it was a good thing most of the officers warnt like them and all that, but he liked flying a lot, so we went on most of the missions, not skipping them the way about half the crew did. And I didn't mind it much myself—it warnt much trouble because there warnt nothing to do in the back of the plane but sleep or play cards or set there and watch the country go under you. Finally I got a checkerboard and took that along, and me and Ben and this other fellow took turns playing each other, only the other fellow didn't play much because he was working on a model airplane that he took along with him. We never did get to know him too good, though, because he finally just quit coming altogether, and I guess he must have dropped off the crew because we didn't see him around nowhere for a long time.

Anyhow, there warnt much to it; when we was scheduled for a mission, me and Ben went and crawled in the back of the plane, and when it landed, we crawled back out, and never had anything to say to anybody except sometimes when Lieutenant Bridges would call back to see if anybody else was around, and I was kind of enjoying it. And then one day I happened to meet the co-pilot up in Operations, which was a right peculiar thing because we was just standing there talking together and his voice sounded familiar and he said mine did too, and finally we found out we was on the same crew together. His name was Lieutenant Gardella and he seemed like a real nice fellow, and when I asked him what they done up in the front of the plane, he said, "Nothing much. What do yall do in the back?"

So I told him about the checkers and the cards that we played sometimes and he said that sounded mighty good to him and that he would come back and play with us sometimes, and I told him I would like to have him and that I wanted him to meet Ben besides. I asked him what his job was and he said, "Oh, I do different things. Mainly, I just let the wheels up and down and I stick to that pretty much as I dont care to take on anything more right now."

"How long you been letting them up and down?"

"A pretty good while," he said. "About six weeks now, ever since I got out of cadets. Next time we fly I'm going to let the flaps up and down too. Say, why dont you come up front and fly with us next time? Why dont you ask Bridges about it?"

"Well, that's mighty nice of you. I'd sho like to see you let them wheels up and down."

"Sure," he said. "I'll show you all about it."

He was a real obliging kind of fellow that way and you wouldnt think he was an officer at all just to look at him—he looked like he was only about thirteen years old and you would probably think he was a Boy Scout instead of an officer if you seen him, only he always had this big cigar in his mouth and usually didnt seem real sober neither, which of course aint like most Boy Scouts as they usually seem right sober most of the time.

So I went out and finally found Lieutenant Bridges in the BOQ and he was lying down on his bunk and I had to stand around a while before I could tell whether he was asleep or awake with his eyes half open the way they always was, but finally he set up and looked at me, and I told him what I wanted. And he said, "Look here, you cant just go around flying here and there. Why dont you ask your own pilot?"

And I told him *he* was my pilot, and so he looked at me for a while and finally said, "Oh, yeah, I thought I had seen you around somewhere before. What did you say your name was now?"

So we talked for a while and he said I could ride up front with them on the next trip, and then I asked about Ben, and he said, "Ben who?" and I explained to him that Ben was another one of his gunners, and he said it was all right by him, that it didnt make no difference to him one way or the other.

But when I went back and told Ben about it, Ben said, "No, I'll stay in the back where I'm supposed to stay. I never seen officers care as little about things as this bunch does. I wish we had never got off the other crew myself."

So I told him I would ride in the back too, but he said, "No, there aint any use in that. After all, the pilot is in charge of the plane and what he says goes, I guess, even if he dont seem to know what he is talking about half the time."

But they warnt all that bad, I didnt think, and I really enjoyed watching them work when I flew up front. We took off that day about dark and Lieutenant Bridges got the plane off the ground real good and Lieutenant Gardella let the wheels up and done a right good job of it too, right smack up in the sides like he had been borned doing it; we went skimming out over the end of the runway and then Lieutenant Gardella got out a cigar and stuck it in his mouth and rared back and begun reading a magazine, while Lieutenant Bridges flew back over the field and then set it on the automatic, and then propped his feet up and leaned his seat back to go to sleep. I watched it all and it seemed like they done right good, and then I went back to talk with Lieutenant Kendall, the engineer, only he said he was sleepy and was getting his parachute under his head and sticking his feet out in the aisle trying to get comfortable. So I finally went back and set in the radio operators seat, because he hadnt showed up, and watched Lieutenant Cover while he navigated; and he was the one I wished Ben could have seen because he was probably the hardest-working man I ever seen in my life. He was bounding all over the back of the plane navigating even before it was over the end of the runway, peeping down tubes and looking out the window and writing things down on maps that he had scattered all over the desk, then grabbing up one of them three watches that he had scattered around and checking the time, and writing that down, and then taking this camera-looking thing he

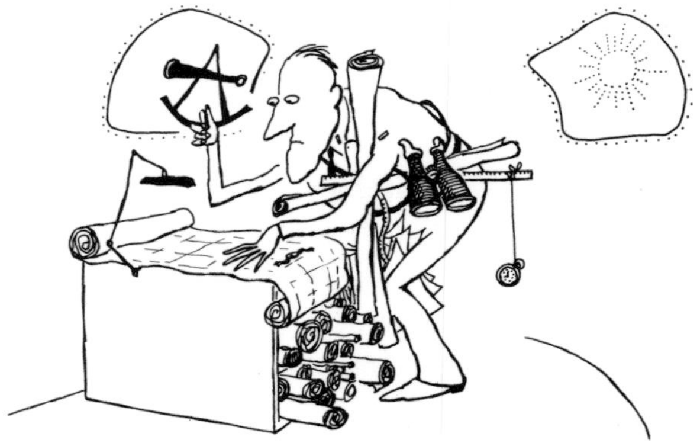

had, and running back to the dome and pointing it out at the stars that was just coming out, and then running back to write that down too. He wrote so fast and so hard that twice the lead flew off the pencil and flipped across the plane and nearly hit me in the eye; and another time he snatched up a map that had this weight on it that sailed across the desk and caught me right beside the head; so I got up and moved down a ways after that as it did seem right dangerous being close to him working that hard but I still watched him a good while and got a kick out of it.

Anyhow, I wished Ben could have seen it the way he went at things; he was so busy most of the time he wouldn't even talk to me. Most people that work hard usually like to talk about it a good bit, but when I asked him where he was navigating to, he snapped real quick, "Biloxi, Mississippi. Dont bother me, I'm busy," and wouldnt even look at me. After a little bit, we was well on the way and it was dark and the plane was quiet the way it gets at night, with only the sounds of the engines and no lights to speak of except little blue dials and the lamp that come down over Lieutenant Cover's head; but watching him work was enough to wear you out, so I got a little bit sleepy, and must have dozed off for a good while because when I woke up there was a big disturbance going on with people walking around and talking, and I didnt know what was going on.

Anyhow, I woke up and felt the plane going in these big circles, and then I looked over to the desk and there was Lieutenant Bridges standing holding one of the maps in his hand and looking at it, and Lieutenant Cover arguing with him, rattling papers around and trying to show him how he had figured this and that. Lieutenant Kendall was setting over there watching them with his chin propped up on his hands, and Lieutenant Gardella was up front flying the plane in these big circles, looking around every once in a while to see what was going on with the big cigar stuck out of his mouth; they was talking loud and everybody seemed real interested in it, and it seemed like Lieutenant Bridges knowed a lot about navigation himself even though he was the pilot. He was waving the map around saying, "I dont care what your figures show. I guess I can look out the window and *see,* can't I?"

"Well, you just check the figures for yourself," Lieutenant Cover said. "I got a fix about thirty minutes ago and that showed us right here, and thirty minutes later, we're supposed to be right *here*. You can check every figure down there. I figured that position by Dead

Reckoning and I figured it thirty minutes from that fix, and I know it's right!"

But Lieutenant Bridges kept on shaking his head and saying, "Well, by God, I can *see,* cant I? I can look right out the window and *see,* cant I?"

So they talked a good bit about navigation that way and both took a lot of interest in it, it seemed like. Lieutenant Kendall was setting back there listening to the whole thing and he was right interested too, even though he was the engineer, and so I stepped back there and asked him what the discussion was all about. And he said, "What do you think it's about? They're lost again naturally. I been in this plane seven times and five of them we been lost. All I know is how much gas we got and if they want to know that, I'll be glad to tell them, but I aint going to worry about it anymore. They can ditch the plane or jump out for all I care; the only thing I know is about how much gas we got."

Then Lieutenant Gardella called back and asked how much gas *did* we have, and Lieutenant Kendall said, "Tell him we can fly another forty minutes. I dont want to talk with him because every time we do, we get in an argument over where we are, and I'm tired of talking about it."

"I know what you mean," I said. "I dont like to argue about things neither, but it is good to see everybody taking such an interest in things; old Ben would be surprised to see it."

"Who is Ben?"

"He's one of the gunners," I said. "He rides in the back of the plane."

"Well," Lieutenant Kendall said. "I hope he knows how to use a parachute."

"Sho," I said. "I bet Ben knows about as much about parachutes as anybody you ever seen."

Anyhow we chatted a while and then I went back and listened to Lieutenant Bridges and Lieutenant Cover some more. Lieutenant Cover was still talking about his DR position where he said we ought to be; he turned to Lieutenant Bridges and said, "Well, who's been navigating, you or me? I got a fix no moren thirty minutes ago and that means our DR position is right here, about a hundred miles out over the Gulf of Mexico . . ."

And then Lieutenant Bridges came in with *his* side of the argument, saying, "Well, I might not have been navigating but I got eyes in my head, and I guess I can look out the window right now and see we're circling over a town half the size of New York; and according to this map or none I ever saw in my life, there aint a town at *all* in the middle of the Gulf of Mexico, much less one half the size of New York and . . ."

"Well, just look then," Lieutenant Cover said. "Dont argue with me, just look. You can check every figure I got here. My DR position puts . . ."

"Well, I dont care anything about that," Lieutenant Bridges said. "All I want to know is what town we're circling over, and if you can tell me that, we can land this thing because we cant fly here all night long while you try to tell me there is a town of that size in the middle of the Gulf of Mexico!"

So they took on that way for a while, and then Lieutenant Gardella and Lieutenant Kendall had a pretty good argument about one of the engines going out; so they discussed that a good while too until Lieutenant Kendall said, "Well, there's not any sense in arguing about it; I'm going to feather the thing." And after a little bit, they changed positions, and Lieutenant Bridges come up front and looked out and seen that one of the engines warnt working, and went back to see Lieutenant Kendall and they had a long talk over the engine being feathered too. Lieutenant Bridges said, "You are not supposed to go around feathering engines like that. I'm the one that's supposed to feather the engine. I'm the pilot, aint I?"

"Yeah, but you was too busy trying to navigate the plane when you're supposed to be up there flying it and . . ."

"All right," Lieutenant Bridges said, "But at least you could have *told* me we had lost an engine. I am the *pilot,* aint I?"

So they talked about that a good while too, and I set back and watched and listened, only I must have dozed off again because when I woke up, we was coming in for a landing. We hit and bounced once pretty hard so that I got throwed halfway across the plane, and then bounced again so that it throwed me back where I started from, but then I grabbed on and didnt get throwed no more on the rest of the bounces. We taxied up the runway with the wheels squeaking and finally stopped and started getting out, but nobody was talking much by then except Lieutenant Gardella—he kept telling Lieutenant Bridges that he thought the *third* bounce was the smoothest of all, but Lieutenant Bridges didnt seem to care about talking about it none, and I noticed in a minute that none of the others did either.

Anyhow, we got out and they had this truck waiting for us and we got on that, and nobody was discussing nothing by this time, and I was right sorry for that because I wanted Ben to hear them because they was right interesting to listen to. But everybody just set there and then Lieutenant Cover come out with all his maps and everything folded up, and he got in and didnt say a word to nobody either. The truck finally started up and we headed across the ramp with everybody real quiet until finally Lieutenant Bridges leaned over and tapped Lieutenant Cover on the shoulder and said, "Look, Cover, I dont mean to run this thing into the ground, but I would appreciate it if you would try to find out where this place is. I mean if it is in the middle of the Gulf of Mexico, we've damn well dis*cov*ered something."

And then Lieutenant Cover said, "Well, the way you fly, it's a wonder we didnt end up there anyhow."

So we drove up and got off and everybody stood around for a while hemming and hawing, and Lieutenant Bridges went over and asked Lieutenant Cover again if he had figured out where we was, and Lieutenant Cover said, "I thought you was the one who knew so much about it. If you want to find out, why dont you ask the driver?"

But then Lieutenant Bridges said, "Ask the driver? You expect me to land a plane and then go over and ask a truck driver where I landed it?" and got right stubborn about it. But then he turned to me and said, "Hey, what was your name now?"

"Stockdale," I said.

"Look, Stockdale," he said. "How about scouting around here somewhere and see if you cant find out what place this is, will you? Be kind of casual about it, you know."

So I went down the way and asked a fellow and he told me Houston, Texas, and I come back and told Lieutenant Bridges and he seemed to feel much better about things then. "Well, Houston aint such a bad town after all," he said. "By gosh, Cover, you're getting better every day. You didn't miss the field but about four hundred and fifty miles this time."

Then Lieutenant Cover said, "Well, what I figured was that you would bounce the rest of the way—it looked like it from the way we landed . . ."

And then Lieutenant Bridges had something to say to that, and after a while they begun squabbling a little bit, which I didnt like to hear. Me and Ben stood around waiting while they went at it and Ben said to me, "I never heered a bunch of officers argue so much in my life!"

"Yeah, Ben, they do now, but you ought to have been in the front of that plane and seen the way they worked. That was something else. If you could have seen that, you would have thought a lot more of them. Why, I'll bet they are about as good a crew as you can find, when they're sober like that."

"Which aint often," Ben said.

Anyhow, I hated for Ben to hear the squabbling and kept on talking to him until they had finished up with it because he got so disgusted about things like that. But they was finally finished; all of them heading across the ramp except Lieutenant Cover who had lost the argument because they had all jumped on him together before it was over—he was getting all his charts and stuff up and mumbling to himself. And I felt right sorry for him the way he had lost out on the argument and everything; I went over to him and said, "Well, I wouldn't worry about it none. I dont see how it amounts to too much. I had just as soon land at this field as any other one, and we aint going to be here but one day nohow. . . ."

But he was right down on things and turned around and looked at me like he was almost mad with me, and said, "Look, do you want to check my figures? Do you want to check them and see for yourself? I got them all right here!"

"Well, I dont know nothing about it," I said. "If you say they're right, I guess they is."

"I can show you my DR position," he said. "It shows us right out in the Gulf."

"Well, I wouldnt know about that," I said. "If you say your DR position is out in the Gulf, I reckon that's where it is all right. How long do you expect it to be out there?"

But he was pretty much down on things; he turned away and stomped off without even answering me—nothing you could say would make him feel any better.